MANAGING LOCAL SERVICES

Books of Related Interest

LOCAL GOVERNMENT REORGANISATION
The Review and its Aftermath
Edited by Steve Leach

QUANGOS AND LOCAL GOVERNMENT
A Changing World
Edited by Howard Davis

FINANCING EUROPEAN LOCAL GOVERNMENTS
Edited by John Gibson and Richard Batley

THE POLITICAL EXECUTIVE
Politicians and Management in European Local Government
Edited by Richard Batley and Adrian Campbell

POLITICS IN AUSTRIA
Edited by Dr Richard Luther and Dr Wolfgang C. Muller

UNDERSTANDING THE SWEDISH MODEL
Edited by Jan-Erik Lane

Managing Local Services:
From CCT to Best Value

edited by

GEORGE A. BOYNE

FRANK CASS
LONDON • PORTLAND, OR

First published in 1999 in Great Britain by
FRANK CASS AND COMPANY LIMITED
2 Park Square, Milton Park, Abingdon, Oxon, OX14 4RN

and in the United States of America by
FRANK CASS
270 Madison Ave,
New York NY 10016

Transferred to Digital Printing 2005

Copyright © 1999 Frank Cass & Co. Ltd

Website: *www.frankcass.com*

British Library Cataloguing in Publication Data

Managing local services: from CCT to best value
1. Municipal services - Great Britain - Finance 2. Municipal
services - Contracting out - Great Britain 3. Municipal
services - Finance - Government policy - Great Britain
I. Boyne, George A.
352.5'3'0941

ISBN 0 7146 5020 X (hb)
ISBN 0 7146 8075 3 (pb)

Library of Congress Cataloging-in-Publication Data

Managing local services : from CCT to best value /
edited by George A. Boyne.
    p. cm.
    ISBN 0-7146-5020-X (hb.) – ISBN 0-7146-8075-3 (pb.)
    1. Local government–Great Britain. I. Boyne, George A.
JS3111.M35 1999
352.14'0941–dc21   99–21019
                                                          CIP

This group of studies first appeared in a Special Issue of
Local Government Studies, Vol.25, No.2 (Summer 1999),
[Managing Local Services: From CCT to Best Value].

Contents

Introduction:
Processes, Performance and Best Value in Local Government

GEORGE A. BOYNE

The Labour government elected to office in 1997 made a manifesto pledge to abolish Compulsory Competitive Tendering (CCT) and introduce a new regime of Best Value (BV) in local government. Initial details of the new policy were provided in the '12 Principles of Best Value' which were published in June 1997. The nature of BV was further developed in green and white papers in the spring and summer of 1998 (DETR, 1998a and b). After several months of uncertainty about the room for a local government bill in the government's legislative programme, space was eventually found for BV in the 1998/9 parliamentary session. The Local Government Association hailed this as a victory for local authorities (LGA, 1998). At the time of writing, a bill to give BV a statutory basis in England and Wales has been published, and it seems likely that all councils will be required to implement the relevant procedures from April 2000. In effect, BV has been placed at the top of Labour's agenda for the 'modernisation' of local government. Other proposals for reform, such as alternative political structures and a new ethical framework, have been included only in draft bills.

The purpose of this volume is to provide an initial interpretation and assessment of the new approach to local service provision. BV is still in its infancy (many would say it remains embryonic), but the main features of the regime are already evident. Moreover, BV is potentially the single most important reform of the management of local services since the introduction of CCT itself. It is therefore timely to ask some preliminary but fundamental questions. What is BV? How does it differ from CCT? What is the role of the pilot programme? What are councils' early experiences of attempting to implement BV? How will success or failure in the achievement of BV objectives be monitored and measured? There are, of course, many other questions about BV that will need to be answered in the years ahead. For example, what are the actual effects of the framework on service

George Boyne, Cardiff Business School

performance, service costs and local democracy and accountability? These are the 'wicked research issues' for the academic community. Even after almost 20 years, the answers to such questions about CCT and other Conservative reforms remain unclear (Boyne, 1998a and b). It would be premature at this stage to attempt to assess the actual effects of BV. Nevertheless, the papers in this volume provide conceptualisations and evidence that lay useful foundations for this difficult task.

The aim of this introductory article is to place the following contributions in a broader context. An attempt is made to remove some of the confusion concerning BV by distinguishing between three meanings of the term. The role of competition in the BV framework is analysed: is CCT being abolished or merely modernised? The nature of the BV pilot programme is outlined, and its potential contribution to the development of the new regime is assessed. The arguments and evidence in the remaining articles are also summarised at relevant points in the discussion.

DEFINITIONS OF BEST VALUE

Best Value is a complex and evolving concept. In their first encounters with the new Labour government in 1997, civil servants were reported to be surprised at the lack of detail that ministers were able to provide on BV (*Local Government Chronicle*, 2 May 1997). Almost 18 months later, when the intention to put the new regime on a statutory basis was imminent, an editorial in the *Local Government Chronicle* argued that 'the onus remains on the government to give councils a clear steer on what Best Value is. The lack of clarity starts at the top' (*Local Government Chronicle*, 13 Oct. 1998). Pilot authorities in particular have invested much time and effort in attempting to discover the meaning of BV. To some extent, this is an inherent feature of the pilot programme. All the details have not been worked out by central government in advance. Rather, the task of clarifying and developing BV has been passed over to the pilots.

At least three distinct but linked definitions of BV can be identified. These refer to organisational performance, organisational processes and the relationship between processes and performance. Each of these definitions is now discussed in turn.

Organisational Performance

The term 'Best Value' can be taken to refer to the level of performance achieved by councils in the provision of services. The government's White Paper on BV (DETR, 1998b) identifies five key aspects of performance: cost, efficiency, effectiveness, quality and fair access. This seems to signal a broadening of the '3Es' framework used by the previous Conservative government. In particular, BV may contain a new emphasis on service quality (widely regarded as missing in CCT) and the fair allocation of services between different groups in the population (for example, between age groups, males and females, ethnic and income groups).

However, there are two reasons why caution rather than celebration is appropriate here. First, the examples of these aspects of performance that are listed in the White Paper suggest that the government's understanding of them is idiosyncratic. Efficiency is conventionally defined as the ratio of inputs to outputs, yet the example given is 'percentage of new benefit claims processed within 14 days', which is clearly a measure of the *speed* of service provision (Boyne, 1997). The term effectiveness is used in the White Paper in relation to the *administration* of a service (for example, 'benefits overpaid as a percentage of total benefit expenditure') rather than the ultimate *impact* on service recipients. Finally, fair access is interpreted in a narrow and technical way: the illustrative example is 'the percentage of claimants surveyed who said the claim form was easy to understand'. A second reason for caution is that the local government bill omits any reference to quality and fair access. Rather, the bill contains several statements that councils will have a duty to ensure a combination of economy, efficiency and effectiveness.

Nevertheless, even if the duty of BV is limited to the 3Es, it includes important innovations in performance management and measurement. The BV framework places a new emphasis on *continuous improvements* in performance, which are 'the hallmark of a modern council, and the test of Best Value' (DETR, 1998b: para.7.1). Furthermore, central government will set *targets* for better local performance. This section of the White Paper is worth quoting at length, because it reveals the potentially centralising effect of the BV performance framework:

> The government will require that as a minimum local authorities set:
>
> - quality targets over five years that, as a minimum, are consistent with the performance of the top 25% of all authorities at the time the targets are set;
> - cost and efficiency targets over five years that, as a minimum, are consistent with the performance of the top 25% of authorities in the region at the time the targets are set; and
> - annual targets that are demonstrably consistent with the five year targets.

This framework of targets will put most pressure on those authorities who are currently performing poorly on both the quality and the efficiency with which they deliver services. However, it is likely to exert pressure on nearly all authorities because very few authorities score very highly on both aspects of performance at the same time. (DETR, 1998b: para.7.14)

These central targets for performance improvement raise a number of questions. First, is it possible to define and measure cost and quality with the clarity and accuracy that will be necessary to make the statutory requirements work in practice? Secondly, is it possible to construct meaningful league tables that properly take account of differences in the circumstances that confront local councils? This will require an adjustment for variations in the 'degree of difficulty' in the provision of services across local areas. The calculations could quickly become as technically complex and politically controversial as those involved in the creation of standard spending assessments. Thirdly, are the improvements in performance that are being sought really achievable, even over a five-year period? The current Audit Commission performance indicators imply that some local authorities perform more than *20 times* better than others (Boyne, 1997). For some councils, the performance change over five years is analogous to requiring football teams that are near the bottom of the third division to gain promotion to the Premier League. Of course, there are examples of such sporting success in a short period, but these are usually the product of a huge investment of resources. It seems unlikely that councils labelled as 'poor performers' will be financially favoured in this way.

Even if these issues can be resolved, the centrally specified targets may distort local authority behaviour and undermine local democratic accountability. A familiar problem with performance indicators is that organisations tend to concentrate on the activities that are measured and monitored (Carter *et al.*, 1992; Smith, 1993). This phenomenon in local government is likely to be reinforced if success in hitting the central targets is a precondition of becoming a 'Beacon Council'. Furthermore, the fact that all councils will have their attention directed to the same performance indicators may lead to a dull conformity rather than the innovation that BV is formally intended to promote.

There is a clear tension between local and central accountability in the BV regime. The duty of BV has been consistently described in government documents as one that is 'owed to local people'. However, the presence of centrally specified indicators and targets may direct the attention of local politicians and managers upwards to the government rather than outwards to local communities.

Organisational Processes

The Best Value legislation imposes a duty on councils not only to secure continuous improvements in performance, but also to follow prescribed processes of service management. Most importantly, local authorities must publish annually a performance plan, and must undertake fundamental reviews of their services.

Performance Plans

The purposes of these documents are for each authority to summarise its corporate objectives and communicate them to the public. A performance plan may be a useful source of information, and has the potential to strengthen local accountability. The content of performance plans will be prescribed by the government under secondary legislation. The Green and White Papers (DETR, 1998a and b) suggest that councils will be required to publish

- details of their current performance (probably for the previous financial year)

- comparisons with the performance of other organisations (which may include not only local authorities but also other service providers)

- targets for performance in the year ahead and in the longer term

- proposals for the achievement of the targets (these proposals are also referred to as 'action plans' in the White Paper).

Performance plans could easily become heavy with data, not least because councils will be obliged to include nationally specified performance indicators (as discussed above) as well as indicators that reflect local objectives. If so, they may be inaccessible and unattractive to members of the general public, and add little to local accountability. One solution to this problem may be to publish two versions of the plan: a long version for consumption by elected members, staff and special interest groups; and a short version for distribution to the local population. A potential problem with this proposal is that the short version could be selective and biased. There may well be a temptation for ruling groups on local councils to emphasise the positive aspects of their performance. The government's White Paper (DETR, 1998b) suggests that performance plans should be audited in order to check the veracity of the data. An audit for political bias, however, is likely to be more problematic.

An additional issue that needs to be resolved is the relationship between performance plans and other plans in local government, for example, community plans, education plans and social services plans. Research by the Local Government Management Board (as yet unpublished) has identified *31* plans that councils have a statutory obligation to produce. Furthermore, many of these planning requirements have been imposed in the last few years. According to Power (1997) the growth of regulation in the public sector in the last decade amounts to an 'audit explosion'. Local authorities can be described as facing a 'planning implosion': they may be in danger of collapsing in on themselves under the weight of planning processes. As the Best Value regime develops, there are likely to be demands for the various plans to be rationalised and integrated.

Service Reviews

When BV processes become mandatory in the year 2000, councils will be required to undertake a 'fundamental performance review' of each of their services, probably at least once every five years. This is in addition to the annual setting and monitoring of performance targets, and the formulation of action plans to achieve these targets. The purpose of these reviews is 'to ensure that continuous improvements to all services are made' (DETR, 1998b: para 7.18). Councils will be expected to make

> early inroads into areas of significant weakness. Where the performance of a service is demonstrably poor by any standards – and the framework of national indicators will highlight these – then authorities will be expected to review that service quickly and effectively ... There will also be a case for addressing some of the stronger areas of performance early, so that the lessons of success can be spread quickly. (DETR, 1998b: para 7.18)

The government intends to prescribe a statutory framework for processes of service review. Each review will be required to contain four main elements:

- *challenge* why and how a service is being provided;
- *compare* performance with the achievements of other organisations;
- *consult* with local taxpayers, service users and the business community;
- use *competition* as a means of enhancing performance.

The contents of the White Paper (DETR, 1998b) suggest that one of these 'four Cs' is more equal than the others. Whereas challenge, compare and consult each have one short paragraph devoted to them, the discussion of the *competition* element of service review continues for over two pages. The government emphasises that 'a requirement to use and develop competition as an essential management tool should not be interpreted as a request to put everything out to tender' (DETR, 17.29). However, four of the six 'tests of competitiveness' that are listed in the White Paper (DETR, 1998b: para 7.29) involve competitive tendering to some extent.

The two tests of competitiveness that are not based on competitive tendering are 'an independent benchmarking report' (which is essentially an extension of the 'comparison' stage in service review), and 'dispose or sell off completely a service' (that is, outright privatisation). The remaining four tests of competitiveness are:

- 'provide a core service in-house and buy top-up support from the private sector' (which would require a tendering process under EU procurement law);

- 'contract out a service to the private sector after a competition between external bidders only';

- 'form a joint venture or partnership following a competition for an external partner';

- 'tender part of a service with an in-house team bidding against private sector and other local authority bidders'.

The BV framework thus contains a continuing emphasis on competition. Indeed, it could be argued that BV strengthens the role of competition in local government because it involves all services rather than the defined list of services covered by the CCT legislation. As the White Paper makes clear,

the key strategic choice for authorities is whether to provide services directly themselves or to secure them through other means. The key test is which of the options is more likely to secure best value for local people. Services should not be delivered directly if other more efficient and effective means are available ... retaining work in-house without subjecting it to real competitive pressure can rarely be justified. (DETR, 1998b: 7.28)

The tone and content of government statements to date strongly imply that 'real competitive pressure' is largely synonymous with competitive tendering.

This is not to argue, however, that BV is simply CCT by another name. Despite the remaining role for competitive tendering, there are important differences between the two regimes. In particular, there is a new emphasis on 'fair competition', which refers largely to greater protection of the rights of local authority staff. Under Part II of the 1988 Local Government Act, local councils are prohibited from taking account of 'non-commercial' considerations when awarding competitively tendered contracts. For example, local authorities cannot discriminate between bidders on the basis of their record on equal opportunities or staff training, nor insist on minimum pay levels if a tender is won by an external organisation. The local government bill provides the Secretary of State with powers to relax these constraints. Local authorities may regard this part of the legislation as potentially creating the 'level playing field' that they have long sought in competing with external organisations. Private contractors, on the other hand, may believe that the balance has been tipped against them. As is argued in the White Paper, 'the task of local government will be to combine reassurance to employees with the necessary flexibility to allow transfer on a fair basis to other employers where this is in the public interest' (DETR, 1998b: para 7.24).

The first two papers in this volume explore some of the issues raised by the role of competitive tendering within the BV framework. The abolition of CCT may lead to new contractual relationships in local government. In particular, the 'transactional' style of contract management that characterised CCT may be replaced by 'relational' contracts. This issue is explored in the article by Bruce Walker and Howard Davis. They draw on principal-agent theory, and argue that transactional features of relations between clients and contractors under CCT include detailed contract specifications and highly formalised procedures for monitoring and inspection. Such characteristics arise from the lack of certainty that the relationship between principals and agents will continue beyond the existing contract. By contrast, relational contracts are based on mutual trust and an expectation of a long-term exchange between the parties.

Walker and Davis identify nine conceptual differences between transactional and relational contracts, and proceed to examine empirically the nature of existing contractual relationships in local government. Their results suggest that, in general, both clients and contractors would prefer a more relational style of contract management. In this respect, the extra flexibility that is potentially offered by BV may lead to more productive relationships between principals and agents. However, Walker and Davis caution that mutual trust can degenerate into collusion for private gain and, in some cases, outright corruption. The implication is that a widespread shift to relational contracts would be inappropriate. Some elements of transactional rigidity will need to be retained in order to promote clarity and probity in the relationship between principals and agents. As Walker and Davis conclude, 'there is little likelihood that the looser, more informal, contracting that characterises some parts of the private sector would prove acceptable when set against expected standards for the conduct of public life'.

The retention of competition within the BV regime reflects the Labour government's belief that CCT had some positive effects (DETR, 1998a and b). Local authority accountants' perceptions of the nature and extent of these effects are analysed in John Wilson's contribution. The survey results show general opposition to the extension of competitive tendering to white-collar services, and a strong rejection of the enabling model of local government. Such evidence suggests that a continuing emphasis on competitive tendering in the BV regime is likely to be resisted by local government staff. Indeed, the emphasis on competition could undermine the 'local ownership' of BV that the government is keen to promote.

The Impact of Processes on Performance : Rational Planning Revisited

The connection between BV processes and performance has not been made explicit in government documents. Nevertheless, the clear assumption is that fundamental reviews, target setting and performance plans will collectively lead to the continuous improvements in services that the government is seeking. This is tantamount to a belief that *rational planning* leads to better organisational performance. The processes required to fulfil the duty of BV are consistent with a simple planning cycle that consists of the following stages:

1. review current objectives and performance;

2. set targets for future performance;

3. select a course of action to achieve the targets;

4. monitor progress, and begin again at stage 1.

One of the Blair government's favourite slogans, which is intended to indicate that it has rebuffed dogmatism and embraced pragmatism, is that 'what counts is what works'. The BV framework itself, however, may be regarded as reflecting a dogmatic approach to local service management. The duty of BV refers not only to improvements in performance, but to a particular *method* of securing these improvements. The government appears to be so confident that 'what works is rational planning', that alternative approaches to strategic management, such as logical incrementalism (Quinn, 1980), are ruled out. What justification is there for prescribing rationalist rather than incrementalist processes in local government?

Some support for the emphasis on rational planning can be found in empirical studies of the determinants of performance in the private sector (Boyd, 1991; Miller and Cardinal, 1994). Around 50 statistical analyses of the relationship between planning and the financial success of private firms have been published. The balance of the evidence suggests that, on average, organisations perform better if they follow the rational model (Boyne, 2000). However, planning is not a *necessary* condition of high performance – some firms that simply 'muddle through' are high performers. This is consistent with traditional views on incrementalism in the public administration literature (Lindblom, 1959; Wildavsky, 1973). Nor is planning a *sufficient* condition for success – some private organisations that pursue rational processes are commercial failures. Such evidence suggests that the impact of rational planning on performance may vary with the external and internal circumstances of organisations. In other words, the effectiveness of planning is contingent on other variables. Therefore, even if the BV processes that are prescribed in the White Paper (DETR, 1998b) lead to better performance across local government as a whole, in some councils the imposition of these processes may lead to poorer performance.

A positive connection between BV processes and BV outcomes is also called into question by research on the previous major attempt at rational planning in local government – the 'corporate revolution' in the 1970s. The parallels between corporate planning and the BV framework are very close. For example, Hambleton (1978: 45) argues that a corporate approach involves the development of processes that allow a local authority 'to plan, control and review its activities as a whole to satisfy the needs of the people in its area to the maximum extent consistent with available resources'. Similarly, Greenwood *et al.* (1976: 31) define corporate planning as involving the

> strategic analysis of problems, focusing upon the local authority as a whole, and also issue analysis relating to a more limited area of the local authority's activities ... The aim is an explicit policy making system with a systematic process of policy review, the explicit identification of the authority's objectives, the exposure of the contribution of difference parts to the same objectives, and a concern with performance through output measurement.

Corporate planning in local government 'attained a level of respectability and acceptance almost without parallel in the British public sector' (Gay, 1982: 349). However, many studies have drawn attention to the technical and political problems associated with this approach to policy making. In particular, the data required for the planning process were often lacking, elected members believed that they were excluded from important decisions, power appeared to be unduly concentrated at the centre of authorities, and planning activities were decoupled from the operational realities of service provision (Clapham, 1984; Cockburn, 1977; Dearlove, 1979; Haynes, 1978). Corporate planning was eventually defeated by such problems, perhaps because the procedures were voluntary. Although authorities were encouraged to adopt the corporate approach by central government, there was no compulsion. Perhaps it was too easy to discard the planning processes when the initial problems appeared. It remains to be seen whether the mandatory rational planning imposed by the BV legislation will be more durable and more successful.

THE ROLE OF THE PILOT PROGRAMME

Best Value is being piloted in 23 Welsh and 37 English authorities. The pilot programme covers a range of single-service and cross-service issues, and includes both internal functions (for example, central support to committees) and front-line functions (across the whole range of local government activities). Some pilot authorities are testing the BV framework on one service or a part thereof (for example, residential homes in social services), while others are 'whole-authority' pilots. Most of the latter group are implementing BV across 20 per cent of their functions in the first year, which is similar to the approach that will be required of all councils when 'full scale' BV is introduced in 2000.

In principle, the pilot programme could serve one or more of three main purposes:

1. to evaluate whether BV is worth introducing or not. Put bluntly, does BV work? Do the benefits outweigh the costs?

2. to assess the relative effectiveness of different parts of the BV framework, and to identify whether some parts should be retained and others rejected. For example, does the imposition of performance targets actually lead to better performance? Similarly, in fundamental performance reviews, are all of the four Cs equally useful? Is it worthwhile spending time and effort on comparing performance with other organisations if all services are to be subjected to competitive tendering?

3. to guide local choices on different approaches to BV processes – for example, which methods of consulting the public and of benchmarking appear to work best? What organisational structures and analytical procedures are most likely to lead to genuine challenges to current patterns of service provision?

In practice, the first and second sets of questions are largely beyond the scope of the pilot programme because they are resolved by the local government bill. The primary legislation will be passed long before the pilots can yield comprehensive information on the impact of the BV framework, or on the usefulness of its various parts. The main contribution of the pilot programme will therefore be limited to the third set of questions. The results of the pilots may be used to inform the secondary legislation that will determine *how* not *whether* BV is implemented. The speed and direction of BV is driven, unsurprisingly, by the demands of the political process rather than the needs of the research process. Thus the BV pilot programme does not constitute 'evidence-based policy making' in the full sense. Nevertheless, the pilot process is a clear advance on the 'perverse piloting' that was practised by the previous government. The Conservatives' interpretation of the experimental method was to test a new policy in one area (for example, the poll tax in Scotland), and then, if the results were *negative*, to implement it nationwide.

The general characteristics of the pilot programme and local authorities' early experiences with BV are analysed in five of the articles in this volume. Steve Martin examines the process of selecting English BV pilots, and identifies the main characteristics of the 37 winning bids. These pilot authorities have been exempted from CCT, and a further 16 councils whose bids were 'near misses' have been rewarded with selective exemptions. This incentive for councils to bid for pilot status may have led to a bias in the pilot programme. Local authorities that were especially eager to escape from CCT are more likely to have submitted pilot bids. The pilots are unrepresentative of English local government in other ways. For example, Martin shows that London boroughs and unitary authorities are over-represented in the pilots, whereas non-metropolitan districts are under-represented. Furthermore, the pilots were explicitly selected on the basis of commitment to, or experience of, BV principles and processes. All of these sources of potential bias suggest that caution will be necessary in generalising from the results of the BV pilots to local government as a whole. As Martin concludes, 'the pilot programme reflects a number of important political imperatives at least as much as the desire for a rigorous programme evaluation'. These political imperatives include building support for BV, and 'changing the culture' of local government.

The distinctive characteristics of BV in Wales are highlighted in the article by Boyne *et al.* The pilot programme is building on the close relationship between the Welsh Office and Welsh councils, which has become even closer since Labour gained office (for example, similar annual increases in central funding were denounced by local government as derisory under the Conservatives, but are now welcomed as generous under Labour). All but one of the Welsh Unitary authorities is a BV pilot, and the pilot programme is being steered jointly by the Welsh Office and the Welsh Local Government Association. In Wales, CCT has been suspended since preparations for local government reorganisation began in earnest in 1994, so this source of selection bias in the set of pilots is absent. After summarising and analysing the characteristics of the Welsh pilots, Boyne *et al.* proceed to assess the prospects for the implementation of BV. In particular, they argue that some elements of service review are likely to develop more rapidly and effectively than others, depending on councils' prior knowledge of them. For example, local authorities already have experience of user consultation (partly because of statutory obligations to consult on services such as housing), but benchmarking is 'new technology' to most managers. An implication is that service reviews in the pilots may not cover the full range of information sources, and that action plans for continuous improvement could be biased accordingly. Thus, as in the English case, considerable care will be needed in drawing lessons from the pilots.

The development of BV in Scotland is critically appraised in the article by Arthur Midwinter and Neil McGarvey. There is no pilot programme in Scotland – all 32 unitary authorities are implementing the new policy and are required to demonstrate that BV processes are in place. Midwinter and McGarvey emphasise that BV builds directly on the prior policies of CCT and performance management. They argue that BV 'has taken the positive and negative lessons learned from CCT and performance-related exercises and moulded together a local government best practice model of management'. An important message of Midwinter and McGarvey's article is that BV processes are only one influence on service standards. A more fundamental constraint on organisational performance is the level of financial resources, which 'remains unaddressed' in Scottish local government (and, indeed, in England and Wales). The Labour government would no doubt argue that BV itself can ease the problem of resource scarcity. Hilary Armstrong, the local government minister at the DETR in England, has described BV as 'an opportunity for councils to make annual efficiency savings of 2%' (*Local Government Chronicle*, 4 Nov. 1998). If this interpretation were correct, then local taxes (which currently fund around 20 per cent of local authority spending) could be reduced to zero within the next ten years!

The final two articles in this volume are case studies of responses to BV by local authorities. Dean Bartlett *et al.* analyse the initial impact of BV on two English local authorities, with particular emphasis on the shift from CCT. Even at an early stage, technical and political difficulties in implementing BV were emerging (for example, absence of the information required to undertake meaningful comparisons, and resistance to the new policy by elected members and staff). Nevertheless, Bartlett *et al.* find that BV may create conditions that are favourable to organisational learning. For example, councils are more willing to share information than they were under CCT. The case studies in Bartlett *et al.*'s article also show that, in the early stages at least, councils had discretion to interpret and develop BV in their own way. The absence of detailed central guidelines created confusion, but also generated the conditions for innovation.

A practitioner perspective on BV is provided in the article by Brian James and Joseph Field, who are chief officers in Torfaen County Borough in South Wales. This is a particularly interesting case study for two reasons. First, Torfaen is part of both the English study of BV pilots (funded by the DETR, and undertaken by Warwick Business School) and the Welsh study (funded jointly by the Welsh Office and Welsh Local Government Association, and undertaken by Cardiff Business School). Secondly, Torfaen is a whole-authority pilot: in 1998/99 it is reviewing 21 separate services which constitute roughly one-fifth of its total activities. James and Field analyse the new organisational structures and processes that Torfaen has found it necessary to establish in order to implement BV, and outline the authority's approach to performance planning and service review. The case study provides a valuable insight into the problems of introducing new BV processes, and emphasises the practical difficulties of two of the 4Cs: challenging current patterns of service delivery, and conducting tests of competitiveness. Finally, James and Field draw attention to the potentially adverse effects of the external and internal reporting requirements of BV. As their chief executive, Clive Grace, puts it, the pilot authorities are in danger of 'drowning in process'.

CONCLUSION

The focus of this volume is on BV as a significant innovation in the management of local authority services. This is not to argue, however, that issues concerning BV processes and performance are entirely or even largely *technical*. There are important *political* questions that will need to be resolved as the new framework develops. First, how will the concept of BV be interpreted within each local area? Quite simply, the question is 'best for whom?' The local politics of BV will include struggles between the interests of local authority staff and residents, between service recipients and taxpayers, and between client groups for different services. The emphasis on public consultation and involvement in BV suggests that these issues may be resolved through a new participative politics in local government. This holds the promise of services that are more responsive to local preferences, and a local government system that is reinvigorated by a variety of democratic processes.

Whether this promise is fulfilled will partly depend on the answer to a second political question. How will BV affect the balance of power between central and local government? The new regime contains a large superstructure of checking, monitoring and evaluation. There are to be performance indicators and targets, verification by auditors that BV processes have been followed, and a new power for the Audit Commission to carry out Best Value inspections. In addition, there is the threat that central government hit squads will be used to deal with local councils that appear to be defaulting on their BV duties. The local government bill implies a looser central grip on local finance, but a tighter hold on organisational processes and performance. If the latter elements are pushed too far, then BV, like CCT, may degenerate into a set of rules to be bent or circumvented by councils, rather than a set of principles to be pursued positively.

REFERENCES

Boyd, B., 1991, 'Strategic Planning and Financial Performance: A Meta-Analytic Review', *Journal of Management Studies*, 28, pp.353–74.

Boyne, G.A., 1997, 'Comparing the Performance of Local Authorities: An Evaluation of The Audit Commission Indicators', *Local Government Studies*, 23, 4, pp.17–43.

Boyne, G.A., 1998a, 'Public Services Under New Labour: Back To Bureaucracy?', *Public Money and Management*, 18, 3, pp.43–50.

Boyne, G.A., 1998b, 'Competitive Tendering In Local Government: A Review of Theory and Evidence', *Public Administration*, 76, pp.695–712

Boyne, G.A., 2000, 'Planning, Performance and Public Services', *Public Administration* (forthcoming).

Carter, N., P. Day and R. Klein, 1992, *How Organisations Measure Success* (London: Routledge).

Clapham, D., 1984, 'Rational Planning and Politics: The Example of Local Authority Corporate Planning', *Policy and Politics*, 12, pp.31–52.

Cockburn, C., 1977, *The Local State* (London: Pluto Press).

Department of The Environment, Transport and the Regions, 1998a, *Improving Local Services Through Best Value* (London: HMSO).

Department of The Environment, Transport and the Regions, 1998b, *Modern Local Government – In Touch With The People* (London: HMSO).

Gray, C., 1982, 'Corporate Planning and Management: A Survey', *Public Administration*, 60, pp.349–55.

Greenwood, R. *et al.*, 1976, *In Pursuit of Corporate Rationality* (Birmingham: Institute for Local Government Studies).

Hambleton, R., 1978, *Policy Planning in Local Government* (London: Hutchinson).

Haynes, R., 1978, 'The Rejection of Corporate Management in Birmingham in Theoretical Perspective', *Local Government Studies*, 4, 2, pp.25–38.

Lindblom, C., 1959, 'The Science of Muddling Through', *Public Administration Review*, 19, pp.79–88.

Local Government Association, 1998, *Briefing on the Local Government Bill* (London: Local Government Association)

Miller, C. and L. Cardinal, 1994, 'Strategic Planning and Firm Performance: A Synthesis of More Than Two Decades of Research', *Academy of Management Journal*, 37, pp.1649–65.

Power, M., 1997, *The Audit Society* (Oxford: Oxford University Press).

Quinn, J., 1980, *Strategies for Change: Logical Incrementalism* (Homewood, IL: Richard D. Irwin).

Smith, P., 1993, 'Outcome Related Performance Measures', *British Journal of Management*, 4, pp.135–51.

Wildavsky, A., 1973, 'If Planning is Everything, Maybe it's Nothing', *Policy Sciences*, 4, pp.127–53.

Perspectives on Contractual Relationships and the Move to Best Value in Local Authorities

BRUCE WALKER and HOWARD DAVIS

This article is concerned with the nature of the contracting relationship in local authorities. After considering some of the implications of a basic model of contracting (principal-agent theory) and questioning some of its implications, we briefly examine whether the Compulsory Competitive Tendering (CCT) regime is likely to have forced many clients and contractors into the more adversarial style of contract management that the theory predicts. We then assess the degree to which parties to local authority contracts act, or wish to act, in a more relational manner and consider some of the implications of the Best Value regime. We conclude by suggesting that there are some important requirements which need to be placed upon public sector contracting behaviour to limit the implementation of 'full' relational styles in practice.

THE PRINCIPAL-AGENT APPROACH TO CONTRACTING: PRINCIPLES AND PRACTICE

Consider, first, some of the implications of the principal-agent (hereafter, P-A) approach to the analysis of contracting where, in a local authority context, the principal, P, can be seen as the client and the agent, A, can be conceived of as the contractor. The main features of the P-A approach to contracting are well known (see, for example, Sappington, 1991; Petersen, 1995, for valuable summaries) and we make no attempt to repeat them here. Rather, we concentrate on the implications of received P-A analysis that are particularly pertinent to the concerns of this article.

Much of existing P-A theory is concerned with the search for optimal incentive and governance structures under contracting. Arguably, the reason why this occupies such a central role in P-A analysis is that, given that most

Bruce Walker, University of Birmingham; Howard Davis, University of Warwick contracts cannot cover every contingency, A will behave in an entirely self-interested manner and to the detriment of P if such incentives and structures fail to align or constrain A's behaviour to P's requirements. In short, it is assumed that A will behave opportunistically, defined in Williamson's now famous phrase as 'self-interest seeking with guile' (Williamson, 1985: 47), if a chance to do so presents itself. Even the existence of apparent trust in contractual relationships can be interpreted as a careful calculation of risk (Williamson, 1996: Ch.10) while the importance of A's reputation as an agent in apparently mitigating opportunism can be treated simply as the appreciation by A that personal benefit maximisation is achieved by treating contracting as a multi-period, rather than a one period, game (Kreps, 1990). Thus, the sort of contractual relationships predicted by a P-A theory, based on the struggle for individual, as opposed to mutual, benefit maximisation, are likely to be adversarial in nature and based on a low level of trust between the contracting parties.

The difficulties occasioned by self-seeking behaviour within the contract relationship will be compounded by any problems associated with the measurability of, particularly, A's activity. For example, consider the situation where A is contracted to produce an output for the principal P and output depends on both A's own efforts and the 'state of the world' in which A is working. If neither A's efforts nor the given state of the world are accurately measurable by P, variations in A's output, likewise, cannot be accurately ascribed by P to actual or supposed changes in either or both of these factors. Consequently, there is a danger that the incentives offered by P to A may become misaligned, as A is under- or over-rewarded by P for changes in output levels that are not a result of changes in A's own efforts. Existing P-A theory offers some solutions to this, however, particularly if the probability distribution of the exogenous, 'state of the world' variable is known (see Lyons, 1996, for an excellent summary).

What would appear, *prima facie*, to be a second set of issues arises when at least some aspects of the output produced by A are themselves not amenable to measurement, giving rise to obvious difficulties in gearing incentives to reflect the significance of these unquantifiable dimensions of the output produced. However, this problem is not intractable in many instances, at least in a private sector context. One possibility is for A to purchase or lease from P the right to produce the output and to retain any net revenues to which the output gives rise. Even where the price of the output has been fixed by agreement with P, these net revenues will vary directly with the desirability of the measurable/unmeasurable mix provided. Hence, A is given an incentive to produce the optimal mix that P or the direct consumers of the output require. Franchising arrangements, for example in hamburger chains, contain many of the features of such a scheme.

A number of factors can, however, reduce the efficacy of such a franchise-type of solution in a public sector context, even at the level of abstraction at which we are considering them here. To see this, recall that the local authority is P, the client, and A is the contractor, in-house or private. In this situation, in the perceptions of consumers, and indeed in law, P remains responsible for the optimal or appropriate provision of the good or service. Consequently, P will retain a direct, rather than indirect, arm's length interest in the performance of A. Further, in many instances consumers of public services do not pay directly for the output provided by A and/or have little opportunity to purchase from suppliers other than A, so that any market signals received by A through the revenues received from supplying the good may be a poor indicator of the desirability to consumers of the output provided. Since these conditions are likely to obtain in the context of local authority services, as well as in 'internal' contracting in other public services such as health (see, for example, Propper, 1995), it is likely that P, the local authority, in its own interests will need to be aware of, and hence wish to monitor actively, the day-to-day performance of its contractor, A.

However, while attempts to monitor the output or effort of A can be seen as a rational response by P to the problem of ensuring appropriate performance, such monitoring can in itself affect A's performance. Consider a situation where at least some aspects of A's output or general performance cannot be measured directly or indirectly (for example, through performance indicators) by P. As, for example, Whynes (1993) has shown, the introduction of a monitoring regime targeted, inevitably, on those measurable aspects of the task, can lead A to substitute effort towards those aspects of the task which are monitored and away from those not so monitored. He also demonstrates that it is possible for A to improve his or her own welfare by such an action, while P, receiving now a different measurable/unmeasurable output mix, is no better off than before. Indeed, if, as in the case of local authority services delivered to the public, P is not the end user of the output provided by A, the resultant output mix may be inferior for P's 'constituents'.

Such potentially distortionary effects of 'partial' monitoring may also affect the *level* as well as the *mix* of output through the impact on A's motivations. This is an area which has received increased attention in the literature recently (see, for example, Frey 1993; 1997; McMaster, 1995), and, again, we do not attempt a full review here. Its importance for understanding contracting under both CCT and the proposed Best Value regime, which we discuss below, is that increased or significant levels of monitoring can break the 'implicit "psychological contract"' (Frey, 1993: 664) between P and A and crowd out work effort. This is particularly likely, according to Frey (1993: 664 ff) when monitoring or increased regulation or supervision forces A to do what s/he would have done anyway, where A feels that any special effort or dedication that was previously applied to the task is now not appreciated or where self-determination and discretion, or self-evaluation, are reduced. In short, where: *'intrinsic motivation* is crowded out … the overall outcome of an external intervention [through monitoring] may well be against the principal's interests' (Frey, 1997: 436 – emphasis added).

It is important, of course, not to exaggerate the likely effects of monitoring and supervision, or the introduction of a competitive regime, on A's performance. Such effects are, arguably, likely to be felt primarily in tasks where (previously) A was able to exercise discretion and a degree of independence, and these conditions, it might be suggested, obtain more in white-collar than blue-collar activities. Even in this respect, however, Holmstrom and Milgrom (1991) observe that incentives tied to performance are 'so much less common than one-dimensional [P-A] theories would predict' (p.26). They demonstrate that whenever a task is multi-dimensional or interacts with other tasks there is a much wider range of incentive and constraint schemes open to P – including the imposition of bureaucratic rules on A's behaviour (Holmstrom and Milgrom, 1991: 42–3: see also Tirole, 1994) – which can be much more efficient than schemes which relate payment directly to A's output. It also needs to be borne in mind that many blue-collar tasks in a local authority context are in practice multi-dimensional – for example, the courtesy with which refuse collectors deal with householders or the manner in which workers engaged in housing maintenance care for their tools and equipment, when bonus systems frequently operate on speed of job completion (Walker, 1993: Ch.8), are both important aspects of their respective tasks. Hence, it is not clear that the adverse effects that 'excessive' monitoring can have on contractor performance are limited solely to professional services.

We have discussed elsewhere (Davis and Walker, 1997; 1998), as have others (Darwin, 1997; Flynn, 1997) in similar vein, how local authority contracting under CCT exhibits many of the features of the adversarial, client–contractor relationship that the P-A theory outlined above predicts. These features include highly detailed contract specifications and agreements on pricing, and significant monitoring, supervision and inspection (Walsh and Davis, 1993: 99 ff; MacIntosh and Broderick, 1996). However, we have gone on to argue that this may be due less to the essential self-interestedness of the participants than to the regulatory requirements of the CCT regime which tend to enforce that particular type of behaviour. For example, the inability of clients to commit to DSOs beyond the length of the existing contracts or to enter into significant post-tender negotiations with in-house contractors, and the necessity of many DSOs to meet a rate of return specified by central government can lead to working relationships that may reflect those predicted under standard P-A theory even if the motivations of clients and/or contractors are, at root, different from those assumed in the theory (see Davis and Walker, 1998, for a fuller discussion). It can thus be suggested that the introduction of competition for local authority services in the form chosen by the previous government has forced local authority clients and contractors to behave in an adversarial manner. McMaster (1995), for example, has argued that CCT itself, rather than solely the increased monitoring and supervision that normally accompanies it, can have adverse effects on the quality and level of A's output by cutting across the local authority's culture and conventions which had previously encouraged superior levels of performance. As he puts it: '[I]ncreasing the role of the price mechanism without due regard to established conventions … could entail adverse motivational and performance effects. Production costs might fall, but so too will benefit flows' (McMaster, 1995: 424).

Indeed, it can be further argued (Darwin, 1998; Davis and Walker, 1997; 1998) that, in order to increase competitive behaviour in the public sector, central government has forced institutions such as local authorities to adopt models of private sector behaviour:

> which have already been rejected in significant parts of the private sector (including … compulsory and *transactional* contracting), while the [private sector] has been adopting the practices which should have long been an integral part of public sector management …, including … *relational* contracting. (Darwin, 1998: 3–4 – emphasis added)

Hewitt and Bovaird (1996) suggest, similarly, that:

> It … almost appears that the two sectors have passed each other in the night, one [the public sector] seeking the 'old testament' paradise of salvation by market competition, the other [the private sector] seeking the 'new testament' Holy Grail of salvation by collaboration, with the irony that each is seeking desperately what the other has only recently given up. (13)

It is to the importance of different forms of contracting and, in particular, to the 'transactional'/'relational' distinction and its significance for local authorities that we now turn.

TRANSACTIONAL AND RELATIONAL CONTRACTING

A transactional approach to contracting derives from treating the transaction(s) with which the contract is concerned as discrete, economic exchanges conducted formally and as 'engaging only small segments of the total personal beings of the participants' (Macneil, 1974: 693). Such an approach need not necessarily be adversarial, since one-off purchases and short-term market trading relations can be transactional and still yield gains to both parties as in, for example, a single purchase by a consumer from a retailer. However, the possibilities for conflict are significant under such contracting where parties to the transaction approach it in an exclusively self-seeking manner and see themselves as being involved in a zero-sum game – in short, where they behave as they are assumed to behave in the basic P-A model discussed above. In contrast, a relational approach to contracting 'entails long term social exchange between parties, mutual trust, interpersonal attachment, commitment to specific partners, altruism and co-operative problem solving' (Duberley, 1997: 2).

Both Macneil (1974) and Sako (1992) have sought to specify the main characteristics of transactional and relational contracts, though Sako uses somewhat different terminology in her analysis. Taking up her initial discussion of the differing nature of such contracts (Sako, 1992: 9–13), we can identify a number of key dimensions along which differences in contract content and contracting style might be identified. These include:

1. The degree of transactional dependence of A on P and vice versa. Generally, the greater the degree of such *mutual* dependence, the greater the likelihood that the contractual approach is trust-based. If one party, say P, is significantly more dependent on the other (A) than A is on P, then the greater the possibility of A exploiting P, should A choose to act opportunistically, as P is locked into the relationship. Grossman and Hart (1986) have shown that certain patterns of asset ownership can mitigate this problem: one example might be P leasing to A the physical capital necessary for the transaction, so that P can more readily recontract with a different A should the relationship break down. Local authorities leasing, rather than selling, refuse vehicles to a private contractor might be a case in point. Note, however, that 'lock in' only becomes a problem if we assume the less dependent party (A) is going to behave in this self-seeking manner.

2. The nature of the procedures for work ordering. This refers not to the ordering of individual tasks but to the way in which the relationship between P and A is initially set up. More transactional forms of contracting tend to involve pre-contract bidding from a number of potential suppliers with prices agreed before the commencement of the contract itself. More relational contracts may involve directly commissioning work from a known contractor with pricing and other aspects of the work being agreed subsequent to the choice of contractor. Both the rules of CCT and many authorities' standing orders in respect

of the requirement to seek bids for work over a certain value may preclude this aspect of relational contracting in local authorities.

3. The degree of documentation involved can itself also throw light upon the nature of the contractual relationship. Extensive documentation can be taken as a sign that parties to the contract wish to leave little to chance and are seeking to minimise the possibility of unforeseen contingencies arising. This in turn may suggest that one or both parties do not feel able to trust the other to carry out the work as required. We note here, however, and return to the point below, that in a public sector context clear evidence, documentary or otherwise, of the way in which the contract relationship is working and should work may not be an unreasonable requirement.

4. The length of the trading agreement. The longer the duration of the contract, the more likely it is that the relationship is of a trust based nature. The act of both parties committing themselves to a lengthy, rather than a short term or 'spot' relationship, can in itself be seen as a mutual investment in the relationship. The inability of local authorities to show commitment in this way under CCT regulations when the DLO is involved has been noted above.

5. How contingencies are resolved. Contracts are inevitably 'incomplete' since the 'unpredictability of the future makes it virtually impossible to write a contract covering every eventuality relevant to the obligations of the parties … or to specify enforceable penalties for every instance of non-fulfilment' (Usher, 1992: 154). This is one of the factors which, according to P-A theory, gives self-seeking parties the chance to behave opportunistically and we may also view the highly detailed specifications and contract conditions which are a feature of local authority contracting as an attempt to minimise this incompleteness. However, contingencies are inevitably going to arise and where the relationship is essentially transactional this is more likely to lead to disputes, stand-offs and an attempt by one party to enforce penalties which will be resisted by the other. Under relational contracts, parties 'agree *ex ante* not so much on what will be done in each particular contingency as … on the procedure by which future contingencies will be met' (Kreps, 1990: 119). Such a procedure is likely to include, as a first step, an informal and open approach to solving the problem through reasoned negotiation.

6. Technology transfer and training. Under more relational contracting, we are likely to observe a greater willingness by the parties to share knowledge and expertise in order to enhance contract performance and

output than under more transactional styles of contract management. As an example of how such transfers can become problematic, it is well known that there have been difficulties over the extent to which compatibility of private contractors' IT systems with those of the local authority should be required under CCT, and over granting contractors access to the computerised systems of the authority, particularly when confidential information not pertinent to the particular contract can be also be accessed as a result.

7. The nature of communication channels and the intensity of communication. Relational contracting is likely to involve much more two way P-A communication of an informal nature than will occur under transactional contracting. Contact between the parties will not be limited solely to pre-arranged monthly meetings, say, or to meetings that are arranged only in order to respond to contract difficulties. Rather, on-going contact through telephone calls or impromptu meetings and social events will be taken by both parties as an appropriate way in which to facilitate the operation of the contract.

8. The nature of risk sharing. The sharing of risks will be an important part of any contract. Under transactional contracting, which party will bear which risks and costs under identified circumstances will, as far as possible, be specified in the contract, as will the distribution of any benefits. Conversely, relational contracts, while usually specifying key distributional parameters at the outset, will tend to incorporate procedures under which the bearing of risks arising from contingencies or changes in the context in which the contract is operating will be determined. Such procedures, and indeed the 'spirit' of the contract more generally, are likely to assume an attitude of give and take on the part of both parties.

9. The extent of competence, contractual and goodwill trust. These concepts of trust are important – and indeed can be argued to be central to any form of relational contracting. Sako (1992: 10) argues that contractual trust and competence trust, reflecting, respectively, the expectation that promises will be kept and that the contractual partner is competent to carry out the task, are necessary for any trading relationship to function, be it transactional or relational in nature. Goodwill trust, on the other hand, manifests itself in co-operation, mutual assistance, fairness and an absence of opportunism, and as such is a fundamental feature of relational rather than transactional contracting. Indeed, the terms 'trust-based contracting' and 'relational contracting' can be seen as synonymous.

This analysis of the different aspects of contracting, and that of others, such as Macneil (1974), were influential in our study of the nature of contracting in the local authority sector and of the desire for change by the parties to those contracts. The next section outlines the approach taken in that study.

THE ESRC STUDY OF CONTRACTUAL RELATIONS IN LOCAL AUTHORITIES IN ENGLAND

In addition to the desire to add to our stock of knowledge concerning current contracting relations in the local authority sector, the study had three main objectives. First, to identify and describe the differing relationships which develop under contracting in the sector; second, to identify why they have developed in these ways; and, third, to attempt to draw out the implications for policy and practice for both local and central government.

To achieve these objectives, contractual relationships were examined in ten English local authorities. The contracts included those drawn up under CCT and a small number of those for services which were put out to tender voluntarily, and covered those won by both in-house and private contractors. As well as an analysis of the relevant documentation relating to the contracts and services delivered, interviews were conducted with councillors, client and contractor officers, and the managers of private firms contracted to the authorities.

As part of the interviews, interviewees were asked, where feasible and appropriate, to score along a number of dimensions the client–contractor relationship under the contract(s) with which they were concerned. Table 1 shows the dimensions which respondents were asked to score. These dimensions were intended to distinguish between those relationships which are primarily transactional and those which are more relational in nature. Specifically, these dimensions represent the extremes or poles of the transactional-relational contracting relationship continuum.

It was recognised from the outset that no contract in reality was likely to be entirely relational or entirely transactional. Any contract is likely to have elements of both. Further, some of the dimensions identified in our discussion in the previous section were not taken to be pertinent to this part of the study. For example, we did not ask respondents to score 'work ordering' – point 2 above – for the reasons noted there, and the issue of 'technology transfer and training' – point 6 above – did not transpire to be significant in the contractual relations studied. Further, we explicitly included the '*Measurement*' dimension in order to capture the extent to which respondents saw the contract as primarily and exclusively an economic relationship under which monitoring in these terms was likely to be significant.

TABLE 1
THE POLES OF TRANSACTIONAL AND RELATIONAL
CONTRACT RELATIONSHIPS

Transactional Pole	**Relational Pole**
Communication is limited and formal and [In subsequent tables – '*Communication*']	Communication is extensive and both formal informal
Everything is measured in monetary terms [*Measurement*]	Many aspects are difficult to measure. Parties do not measure them
The beginning and end of the contract relationship are clearly defined [*Beginning/ End*]	The beginning and end, if any, of the contract relationship are gradual
Initial planning is complete and specific – only remote contingencies are not covered [*Initial Planning*]	There is limited specific planning at the beginning
There is little or no bargaining as the contract proceeds [*Bargaining*]	The contract involves extended mutual planning – a 'joint creative effort'
The contract agreement binds the parties totally [*Bindingness*]	The agreement is tentative
Almost no co-operation is required after the start of the contract [*Co-operation*]	The success of the contract is entirely dependent on further co-operation in both performance and planning
Each particular benefit and burden is specifically assigned to one party [*Benefits/ Burdens Assignment*]	There is sharing of both benefits and burdens
Specific rules and rights applicable, usually measured in monetary terms [*Specificity of Rules/Rights*]	Rules and rights are non-specific and non-measurable
No altruistic behaviour is expected or occurs [*Altruism*]	There is significant expectation of altruistic behaviour
Unplanned problems in performance or between parties are not expected. If they occur they are covered by specific rules [*Problems Expected*]	The possibility of problems is anticipated and is dealt with by co-operation

Source: Coulson *et al.*, 1998: adapted.

Our primary interest was to see where along the transactional-relational spectrum the contracts studied lay and how, if at all, this could be explained. The next section presents some of our the results which emerged from this part of our research.

SOME RESEARCH FINDINGS[1]

It is important to note from the outset the relatively small scale of the research. Further, the scores that respondents attached to different aspects of their contractual relationship are, clearly, subjective and qualitative. Two identical scores from two different interviewees can, of course, represent different intensities of feeling and opinion. Consequently, aggregating them and subjecting them to any statistical analysis must be approached with extreme caution. Nevertheless, since our aim was to identify any patterns emerging, it was necessary to bring together the scores attached by respondents to the different dimensions of their contracting relationships.

To achieve this, respondents were asked first to score their *existing* contractual relationship from 0 (at the transactional pole) to 10 (at the relational pole) along the dimensions presented in Table 1. They were then asked to indicate through their scores where on these dimensions the contracting relationship *ought* to be in their view – that is, what the respondents' preferred form of contracting relationship was. Given their different roles under contracting, we might expect the views of clients and contractors also to differ. Table 2 therefore shows separately the scores attached by clients and contractors to the various dimensions of their current contracting relationship.

Bearing in mind the caveats concerning such an exercise, noted above, the results in Table 2 would suggest that clients see their current contractual

TABLE 2
CLIENTS' AND CONTRACTORS' VIEWS OF CURRENT CONTRACT
RELATIONSHIPS (AVERAGE SCORES)

Dimensions of Current Relationship	Contractors (n=14)	Clients (n=11)
Communication	6.6	7.1
Co-operation	8.1	8.3
Bargaining	5.5	7.4
Problems Expected	6.9	6.8
Benefits/Burdens Assignment	6.1	5.6
Altruism	6.4	5.6
Measurement	4.9	5.4
Beginning/End	4.0	6.2
Specificity of Rules/Rights	4.9	3.8
Bindingness	4.1	4.5
Initial Planning	4.4	3.7

relationships as more relational than their contractors in a number of important respects. In particular, the extent of communication and bargaining, the impossibility or undesirability of extensive measurement, and a perception that the contract is not a 'one off' time limited relationship are views held more widely by clients than by contractors. The last of these is particularly interesting since it may imply that clients take a longer term view of the contracting relationship and the possibilities of recontracting than do contractors, who, it would seem, are very aware of the limited period of the current agreement. In contrast, contractors believe that there is more altruistic behaviour – on their part, perhaps – than do clients and, possibly as a result, attach less significance to the rules and rights incorporated in the contract. Overall, the average of the scores aggregated across all dimensions of the relationship gives some support to the view that contractors (average score = 5.6) see the current contractual relationship as more transactional than clients (average score = 5.9).[2] This may be no more than a reflection of where, in the contractors' view, the ultimate power in the relationship lies.

TABLE 3

CLIENTS' AND CONTRACTORS' VIEWS OF PREFERRED CONTRACT
RELATIONSHIPS (AVERAGE SCORES)

Dimensions of Preferred Relationship	Contractors (n=14)	Clients (n=11)
Communication	8.5	8.5
Co-operation	8.4	8.1
Bargaining	8.1	8.1
Problems Expected	7.6	7.1
Benefits/Burdens Assignment	7.4	6.0
Altruism	6.8	6.0
Measurement	6.1	5.3
Beginning/End	4.6	4.7
Specificity of Rules/Rights	5.1	4.1
Bindingness	4.7	3.8
Initial Planning	3.1	2.9

We also examined the similarities and differences between clients and contractors in their views as to how the contractual relationship should be managed. Table 3 shows some findings in this respect. One of the most striking features of the results, in comparison to Table 2, is that on ten out of the 11 aspects of the contracting relationship, contractors would prefer a more relational contracting relationship. The only aspect which contractors would like to be of a more transactional nature is that concerning more complete and specific initial planning. Clients would also prefer more of such planning and would ideally choose a somewhat more binding agreement, with, interestingly, a clearer beginning and end to the contract. Clients would like to see broadly the same amount of co-operation and would attach virtually the same importance to measurement as at present. However, in all other respects clients would prefer a more relational style of contracting.

Perhaps as significant for the future of contracting, the above results suggest that there is broad agreement between clients and contractors as to which aspects of contracting should be more relational and less transactional. Taking those features of the relationship which attract a score of 5.0 or more as indicative of areas where a more relational, trust-based style of working is desired, both sets of contracting parties agree on which aspects those should be. The only exception is that contractors would prefer somewhat less specificity in the contractual rules than the clients, although we might find this unsurprising in some respects. Thus, while the 'intensity' with which clients and contractors would prefer greater relational contracting appears to differ – the average scores in Table 3 are 6.4 for contractors and 5.9 for clients[3] – such a way of working under many aspects of the contract is clearly preferred by both parties.

Having said this it is important to note that not all aspects of the contractual relationship are deemed by respondents to be suited to a more relational method of working. Indeed it is possible, drawing on the results in Table 3, and on our interviews, to suggest that the most preferred type of contracting will incorporate relational, mixed and transactional elements. We can summarise these as follows:

Preferred Relational Aspects – Co-operation and Communication

In respect of relational aspects of contracting, our respondents seem to prefer that:

(1) There should be significant co-operation in both performance and future planning on the grounds that the success of the contract is heavily dependent on such activity.

(2) There should be extensive communication, both formal and informal.

(3) The contractual relationship should be seen as a joint creative effort.

(4) Difficulties are both anticipated and are solved by mutual co-operation.

Preferred Mixed Aspects – Measurement, Assignment and Sharing of Benefits

Our respondents suggest that they prefer some aspects of contracting to be something of a mix of the transactional and the relational. In particular it is felt that:

(5) Considerable sharing of benefits and costs is preferred, but that some benefits and costs should be specifically assigned to one party.

(6) Both parties should have 'reasonable' expectations of altruistic behaviour.

(7) Many aspects do need to be measured in monetary terms but that some cannot be so measured, or, indeed, measured at all.

Preferred Transactional Aspects – The Contract and Its Basic Parameters

Those interviewed indicated that they preferred some elements of the contracting arrangement to be, or to remain, primarily transactional in nature. Specifically, they preferred that:

(8) The beginning and end of the contractual relationship should be clearly defined.

(9) Specific rules and rights concerning the nature of the contract and its management should be agreed, and should be widely applicable.

(10) The contractual agreement should be binding in most of its important aspects.

(11) Initial planning should be as complete and specific as possible so that only remote contingencies are not covered.

Overall, this would suggest that both clients and contractors value the certainty that clear initial specification of the contract with its attendant duties, obligations and expectations can provide. Subject to this, some flexibility and altruism is preferred, and it is felt to be necessary to trust the other party to perform appropriately on those aspects of the contract which cannot be measured. Although almost impossible to specify in a contract, both clients and contractors wish to engage in the sort of extensive co-operation, communication and mutual planning that can only arise under a relational, trust-based contracting relationship.

It is to the implications of the above discussion for the new Best Value regime, particularly the apparent desire for a more relational form of contract management, that we now turn.

CONTRACTING UNDER BEST VALUE

The introduction to this volume discusses the main features of the Best Value regime and that discussion will not be repeated here. Suffice it to say that the present government takes the view that under Best Value competition will remain 'an essential management tool' (DETR, 1998c:

para.7.29). Although the government has indicated that 'retaining work in-house without subjecting it to real competitive pressure can rarely be justified' (DETR, 1998c: para.7.28), it is also suggested that this should not be interpreted as a requirement to put everything out to tender (DETR, 1998c: para.7.29). Thus, Best Value may offer local authorities the opportunity to consider the appropriateness (or otherwise) of contracting for any given service, even if some of the regime's requirements, and the possibilities for external intervention into authorities' activities (see House of Commons, 1998) may prove onerous. Best Value also offers scope for alternative packaging of contracts and for different forms of the contractual relationship. CCT was very prescriptive in these respects and, as its scope was extended, it was increasingly applied to the contracting of services where, arguably, it may have been inappropriate.

We would argue that in considering whether or not to draw up a formal contract, the first task is to achieve a workable definition of the activity to be covered. If it is not possible to produce a workable definition, it will not be possible to monitor service delivery in any meaningful sense. Such monitoring should not be excessive if the problems associated with such an approach, as outlined earlier, are to be avoided. However, whether the contracting style is to be relational or transactional, it still remains the case that if it is not possible to monitor service delivery, then any negotiations over required changes in delivery or any enforcement action that may ultimately be necessary become problematic. Further, finding an appropriate remedy for performance failure or options for performance improvement becomes virtually impossible.

In general, the early CCT services, such as refuse collection, were comparatively straightforward in these respects, even if definition, monitoring and enforcement could often become bureaucratic. Arguably, these are the sorts of services to which many aspects of P-A theory discussed earlier are most readily applicable. The subsequent application of CCT to many other services, however, raised greater problems. Consider, for example, legal services. Essentially, a key element of what an authority requires from its legal service is good legal advice. In practice, this is difficult to define and in the short and medium term it is also difficult for an authority to know whether the advice received is indeed good. If it transpires that it is not, it is even less clear what the appropriate remedy might be. Table 4 illustrates this argument in respect of four services, taking the three criteria discussed above – definition, monitoring and remedy – as a guide to whether contracting for them is likely to be successful.

Since Best Value does appear to offer the possibility of avoiding the inflexible requirements of CCT, where authorities do decide to put a service out to open competition they may be able to, and may wish to, select

TABLE 4
THE POSSIBILITY OF EFFECTIVE CONTRACTING FOR
SOME SELECTED SERVICES

Criteria	SERVICE			
	Refuse Collection	Vehicle Maintenance	Catering	Legal Advice
Can the Service be Readily Defined?	Yes	Yes	Yes	No
Can the Service be Readily Monitored?	Yes	No	Yes	No
Is there an Appropriate Remedy for Performance Failure?	Yes	Yes	No	No

alternative contracting models according to the nature of the service. We would suggest that where the answers to the questions in Table 4 are 'Yes', 'Yes', 'Yes', the 'hard split' transactional contracting which has been a feature of CCT may still be appropriate. However, as the answers move towards 'No', 'No', 'No' then softer, more relational models of contracting may offer attractive and feasible alternatives. As we have seen, both clients and contractors currently operating under local authority contracting arrangements are likely to welcome such a move. Before endorsing this fully, however, it is necessary in our view to sound a cautionary note. This we do in the next section.

RELATIONAL CONTRACTING IN LOCAL GOVERNMENT – SOME CAVEATS

Seal and Vincent-Jones (1997) have summarised one set of concerns about the extension of trust-based, relational contracting to local government services. They argue that:

> [The] positive image of trust that emerges from the literature is based on an implicit assumption that trusting relationships are somehow welfare enhancing. Less obvious are the negative aspects of trust – trust between members of self-serving elites which may flourish within bureaucracies whether they are located in town halls or Communist Parties. (p.7)

In addition, as we have argued elsewhere (Davis and Walker, 1998), it is important to note that, with contracting, motivations change – indeed, they have to. The first objective for a contractor has to be to survive. For local authority services one consequence of this is that a contractor's staff, especially where that contractor is a DLO/DSO, quickly have to learn that they are not there to provide the best possible public service, but that they are there to provide the best possible public service *according to the contract*. A contractor cannot afford to do too many things without charging and survive financially. Ultimately it is the client who must decide what services are to be provided, and how, and to provide the necessary resources for them. This can be argued to work against traditional ideas of public service, as the Committee on Standards in Public Life recognised. The Committee commented that,

> Decentralisation and contracting out have varied the format for organisations giving public service. There is greater interchange between sectors. There are more short term contracts. There is scepticism about traditional institutions. Against that background it cannot be assumed that everyone in the public service will assimilate a public service culture unless they are told what is expected of them and the message is systematically reinforced. The principles inherent in the ethic of public service need to be set out afresh. (Committee on Standards in Public Life, 1995: 17).

The Committee set out 'Seven Principles of Public Life': selflessness, integrity, objectivity, accountability, openness, honesty and leadership (p.14). The first of these, 'selflessness' ('holders of public office should take decisions solely in terms of the public interest'), is undoubtedly undermined by contracting. Openness, honesty and integrity cannot be assumed but must be demonstrated.

On a similar note, the Code of Conduct for Local Government Employees (Association of Metropolitan Authorities *et al.*, no date) notes that:

> All relationships of a business or private nature with external contractors, or potential contractors, should be made known to the appropriate manager. Orders and contracts must be awarded on merit, by fair competition against other tenders, and no special favour should be shown to businesses run by, for example, friends, partners or relatives in the tendering process ...
>
> Employees must be aware that it is a serious criminal offence for them corruptly to receive any gift, loan, fee, reward or advantage for doing, or not doing, anything or showing favour, or disfavour, to any person in their official capacity.

Similar points are made in the Labour Party's Rules for Local Government Labour Groups, which require all Labour councillors 'to uphold the highest standards of probity and integrity' (Labour Party, 1996: rule 13A.12) and go beyond statutory requirements on the registration and declaration of interests.

Even so, there are still claims, such as those made by Freedland (1998), that 'a viscous river of sleaze trickles along the corridors of local government'. He argues that corruption in British local government 'reflects the poverty of our local democracy'. The prime minister has also argued that 'the way local government currently operates is inefficient and opaque' (Blair, 1998: 16) and has stated that 'Councillors and officials that are incompetent or corrupt not only undermine their leadership credentials but sully the reputation of local government as a whole. We cannot and will not tolerate corruption and malpractice' (ibid.: 18). Yet he has also noted that 'Increasingly the pattern will be for authorities to enter into more partnerships and joint ventures with businesses and voluntary agencies, and other public bodies to deliver local services' (ibid.: 20).

The DETR has similarly stressed that, given that there will be no return to the 'somewhat mechanical and inflexible' working (DETR, 1998a: para.4.16) that characterised CCT, a key feature of Best Value will be effective partnership which 'requires a different approach, which reflects the characteristics of the service in question and the preferences of the private and voluntary sectors, as well as service users' (ibid.: para.4.16).

The problem arises in identifying when 'partnership' becomes corruption. In choosing one partner, or a set of partners, we exclude others. The full details of a relationship, and what makes it work successfully, may well be 'opaque' to outsiders. The difficulty is ensuring that such relationships work in the public interest and are seen to do so. Discussions about the influence of Freemasonry illustrate the point. There may be nothing untoward, yet widespread suspicion remains. Seen in this light, some of the more rigid requirements of CCT – and even Best Value – may be in the public interest, even though they give rise to the detailed documentation and specification, and require clear rules on the distribution of costs and rewards, which we have suggested are characteristic of transactional relationships

History shows us that corrupt relationships are by no means unknown in local government. Large amounts of money can be at stake. Freedland (1998) is arguably right in saying that we must 'shed the myth of our own incorruptibility. We have long assumed corruption to be a faraway malady – endemic in Italy or Latin America, but hardly a worry here'. Partnerships, and 'non-transactional' relationships more generally, certainly contain the ingredients for corruption. The closer the partnership or relationship, the greater the potential for corrupt practice. In moving away from the rigid bureaucracy of CCT to more flexible models of contracting, this possibility has to be weighed against the potential benefits of realising more innovative and productive modes of working. It needs to be constantly borne in mind that public services are spending other people's (taxpayers') money, and that what is acceptable in the private domain may be unacceptable in the public domain. Arguably, financial probity and the fiduciary duty that authorities owe to their taxpayers is enhanced and made visible by clients and contractors being able to demonstrate that relations between them are conducted according to clear financial requirements and standards. Too 'cosy' a relationship between clients and contractors can sit uneasily with these requirements.

The DETR's consultation paper on a new ethical framework for local government comments, in this respect, that:

> An essential prerequisite of any ethical framework is that there is clarity as to the standards of conduct. That this is in doubt in local government – in particular in the fundamental area of handling of conflicts of interest – is not satisfactory and must be remedied. People serving in public life in local government need to understand fully what is expected of them. Equally, it must be clear to the public at large what is being demanded of those who are serving them. (DETR, 1998b: para.1.7)

None of this is to deny, of course, that, as we have noted, a greater degree of trust between client and contractor would be beneficial to taxpayers and service users. However, there is little likelihood that the looser, more informal, contracting that characterises some parts of the private sector would prove acceptable when set against accepted and expected standards for the conduct of public life.

CONCLUSIONS

Martin (1993), in considering the challenges raised by CCT, suggests that the major issues are:

> about how to construct a new ethos combining the essential and special role of public service with new forms that improve its performance. How to transform the relationship with service users from one in which they are passively cared or provided for to one in which they can actively participate in designing their service if they wish? How to release and reward individual initiative while strengthening rather than undermining collective security and responsibility? How to respond readily and quickly to the aspirations of service users while ensuring, through an appreciation of the wider needs of the community, and accountability to it, that unrepresentative groups do not capture the "user" constituency? How to balance competition with co-operation and ground it in values that encourage its creative potential while containing its destructive power? How to meet the ever-growing demands on public service without an ever-growing share of society's resources? How to mobilise the

professionalism of public service specialists without succumbing to a tyranny of the professional? (Martin, 1993: 175)

Clearly, some of these points go beyond the contracting question. Relational contracting, however, does go some way to meeting a number of the concerns expressed about CCT and to developing a more partnership-based approach. It allows flexibility to change the nature of a service or a relationship as needs and circumstances change. It allows long term partnerships to flourish. We have, however, also suggested that full relational contracting is not necessarily desirable in the context of the public service. Nevertheless, our research shows a desire among those who have to make local public services work for a move away from the straitjacket approach that has characterised CCT. One of the interviewees in our study put it thus: 'I'd like to see more of a teamwork approach ... where everybody shared the problem.' Best Value offers both this and the opportunity to develop 'horses for courses' through using a variety of models of contracting depending on the nature of the service concerned.

ACKNOWLEDGEMENTS

Earlier drafts of this article were presented as papers to the Public Services Research Unit Conference 'Public Services Under Labour: Markets or Bureaucracy?' at Cardiff Business School, the University of Wales, and the Quasi-Market Research Seminar at the London School of Hygiene and Tropical Medicine, the University of London, in April, 1998. We are grateful to the participants at these conferences for their most helpful comments. Those papers and this article are based on research undertaken into contracting in local government, supported by the ESRC under award number R000 236498. We gratefully acknowledge the ESRC's valuable financial assistance for this work. We would also like to thank our colleagues on the research programme, Andrew Coulson of the Institute of Local Government Studies, The University of Birmingham, and John Darwin, Joanne Duberley, and Phil Johnson of the Change Management Research Centre, Sheffield Hallam University, for their extensive contribution to the research which has done much to influence our own thinking. However, the authors alone remain responsible for the inferences drawn in this article and for any errors arising.

NOTES

1. John Darwin undertook the task of drawing together his and the research team's 'quantitative' results discussed in this section. We are most grateful to him for this work. A fuller discussion and report of this work can be found in Coulson *et al.* (1998).
2. Note that such averages must be treated with extreme caution since they imply that each aspect of the relationship is equally important to the respondents.
3. Recall the caveat attached to such averages noted in note 2 above.

REFERENCES

Association of Metropolitan Authorities *et al.* (no date), *Code of Conduct for Local Government Employees* (London: Local Government Management Board).

Rt. Hon. Tony Blair, MP, 1998, *Leading the Way: A New Vision for Local Government* (London: Institute for Public Policy Research).

Committee on Standards in Public Life (the Nolan Committee), 1995, *First Report*, Cm 2850-I (London: HMSO).

Coulson, A. *et al.*, 1998, *Client–Contractor Relationships in Ten Local Authorities*, Occasional Paper 10 (Birmingham: School of Public Policy, The University of Birmingham).

Darwin, J., 1997, 'The Partnership Mindset', in Montanheiro, L.C., R.H. Haigh and D.S. Morris (eds.), *Understanding Private and Public Sector Partnerships* (Sheffield: Sheffield Hallam University Press).

Darwin, J., 1998, 'Partnership: What Type of Relationship?', *ESRC Research Programme: An Organisational Behaviour Approach to Local Authority Contracting*, Working Paper (Sheffield Hallam University, mimeo).

Davis, H. and B. Walker, 1997, 'Trust Based Relationships in Local Government Contracting', *Public Money and Management*, Vol.7, No.4, pp.47–54.

Davis, H. and B. Walker, 1998, 'Trust and Competition: Blue Collar Services in Local Government', in A. Coulson (ed), *Trust and Contracts: Relationships in Local Government, Health and Public Services* (Bristol: Policy Press).

DETR (Department of the Environment, Transport and the Regions), 1998a, *Modernising Local Government Through Best Value*, Consultation Paper (London: DETR).

DETR (Department of the Environment, Transport and the Regions), 1998b, *Modernising Local Government: A New Ethical Framework*, Consultation Paper (London: DETR).

DETR (Department of the Environment, Transport and the Regions), 1998c, *Modern Local Government: In Touch With The People*, Cmnd 4014 (London: The Stationery Office).

Duberley, J., 1997, 'Factors Impacting Upon the Nature of the Contracting Relationship', *ESRC Research Programme: An Organisational Behaviour Approach to Local Authority Contracting*, Working Paper (Sheffield Hallam University, mimeo).

Flynn, N., 1997, *Public Sector Management* (Hemel Hempstead: Prentice Hall/Wheatsheaf Harvester).

Freedland, J., 1998, 'Britain's Problem With Corruption', *The Guardian*, 4 Feb.

Frey, B.S., 1993, 'Does Monitoring Increase Work Effort? The Rivalry with Trust and Loyalty', *Economic Inquiry*, Vol.31 (Oct.), pp.663–70.

Frey, B.S., 1997, 'On the Relationship Between Intrinsic and Extrinsic Work Motivation', *International Journal of Industrial Organization*, Vol.15, pp.427–39.

Grossman, S. and O. Hart, 1986, 'The Costs and Benefits of Ownership: A Theory of Vertical and Lateral Integration', *Journal of Political Economy*, Vol.94, pp.691–719.

Hewitt, F. and T. Bovaird, 1996, 'Trends in Strategic Purchasing Patterns: A Comparison Between Public and Private Sectors', *International Research Symposium on Public Services Management* (Aston Business School, Aston University).

Holmstrom, B. and P. Milgrom, 1991, 'Multi-Task Principal-Agent Analyses: Incentive Contracts, Asset Ownership, and Job Design', *Journal of Law, Economics and Organization*, Vol.7 (Spring), pp.24–52.

House of Commons, 1998, *Local Government Bill* (London: The Stationery Office).

Kreps, D.M., 1990, 'Corporate Culture and Economic Theory', in J.E. Alt and K.A. Shepsle (eds.), *Perspectives on Positive Political Economy* (Cambridge: Cambridge University Press).

Labour Party, 1996, *Rules for Local Government Labour Groups* (London: The Labour Party).

Lyons, B.R., 1996, 'Empirical Relevance of Efficient Contract Theory: Inter-Firm Contracts', *Oxford Review of Economic Policy*, Vol.12, No.4, pp.27–52.

MacMaster, R., 1995, 'Competitive Tendering in UK Health and Local Authorities: What Happens to the Quality of Services?', *Scottish Journal of Political Economy*, Vol.42, No.4, pp.409–27.

Macneil, I.R., 1974, 'The Many Futures of Contracts', *Southern California Law Review*, Vol.47, pp.691–816.

Martin, B., 1993, *In the Public Interest? Privatisation and Public Sector Reform* (Zed Books).

McIntosh, I. and J. Broderick, 1996, '"Neither One Thing Nor The Other": Compulsory Competitive Tendering and Southburgh Cleansing Services', *Work, Employment and Society*, Vol.10, No.3, pp.413–30.

Petersen, T., 1995, 'The Principal-Agent Relationship in Organisations', in P. Foss (ed), *Economic Approaches to Organisations and Institutions: An Introduction* (Brookfield, Vermont: Dartmouth Publishing Company).

Propper, C., 1995, 'Agency and Incentives in the NHS Internal Market', *Social Science and Medicine*, Vol.40, No.12, pp.1683–90.

Sako, M., 1992, *Prices, Quality and Trust*, Cambridge Studies in Management no 18 (Cambridge: Cambridge University Press).

Sappington, D.E.M., 1991, 'Incentives in Principal Agent Relationships', *Journal of Economic Perspectives*, Vol.5, No.2, pp.45–66.

Seal, W. and P. Vincent-Jones, 1997, 'Accounting and Trust in the Enabling of Long-Term Relations', *Accounting, Auditing and Accountability Journal*, Vol.10, No.3, pp.406–31.

Tirole, J., 1994, 'The Internal Organisation of Government', *Oxford Economic Papers*, Vol.46, pp.1–29.

Usher, D., 1992, *The Welfare Economics of Markets, Voting and Predation* (Manchester: Manchester University Press).

Walker, B., 1993, *Competing for Building Maintenance: Direct Labour Organisations and Compulsory Competitive Tendering* (London: HMSO).

Walsh, K and H. Davis, 1993, *Competition and Service: The Impact of the Local Government Act 1988* (London: HMSO).

Whynes, D.K., 1993, 'Can Performance Monitoring Solve the Public Services' Principal-Agent Problem?' *Scottish Journal of Political Economy*, Vol.40, No.4, pp.434–46.

Williamson, O.E., 1985, *The Economic Institutions of Capitalism* (New York: The Free Press).

Williamson, O.E., 1996, *The Mechanisms of Governance* (New York: Oxford University Press).

From CCT to Best Value:
Some Evidence and Observations

JOHN WILSON

The Labour government has introduced the policy of Best Value (BV) and, in so doing, has abolished the centrepiece of previous Conservative policy towards local government, that is, Compulsory Competitive Tendering (CCT). CCT was designed to effect not only improvements in service delivery but also a cultural change amongst local authority personnel. The ability of local government to respond to BV may be gauged by considering its response to, and the impact of, CCT. This paper focuses on the views of a key group of local authority personnel, finance professionals, and considers the extent to which CCT, as applied to blue-collar and non-finance white-collar services, had a beneficial impact on service delivery and facilitated a change in attitude amongst local government officers.

The Labour government is committed to abolishing Compulsory Competitive Tendering (CCT) and replacing it with Best Value (BV). Although the practicalities of BV have yet to be determined, and the threat of some form of enforced tendering lingers should authorities fail to demonstrate effectiveness and quality in service delivery, there is an opportunity for local authorities to influence the evolution of the initiative. The commitment to abolish CCT reflects the new environment within which authorities are now operating. Both the Labour government and the Conservative opposition are stressing the need for a constructive relationship with local authorities. Blair (1998) has emphasised the importance of establishing a partnership between central and local government. The Conservative leader, William Hague, at the party's annual local government conference in February 1998, stated unequivocally that the party, when re-elected, would return power to local councils and would never again ignore the views of those at local level (see Harding, 1998). The

John Wilson, Liverpool John Moores University

question remains, however, whether local authorities will be able to capitalise on this opportunity for rehabilitation by meeting the challenge of BV.

Their ability to demonstrate BV may be gauged by considering the impact of, and local authorities' response to, CCT and the broader Conservative era 1979–97. Successive Conservative governments sought to empower the users of local services and to increase private sector involvement in the delivery of them. To this end, CCT was a central feature of Conservative policy. It entailed exposing blue-collar and white-collar (or support) services to private sector competition and resulted, *inter alia*, in a shift in power to service users, including, importantly, internal customers, that is, those who use central support services.

Those authorities which responded positively to the Conservative agenda, by pursuing policies not only designed to increase efficiency but also to reduce bureaucracy and to engage with internal and external service users in determining their requirements and preferences, may be better placed to respond to BV. However, although blue-collar CCT has been reasonably well researched (see, for instance, Walsh, 1991; Walsh and Davis, 1993; Boyne, 1998), the impact of white-collar CCT remains largely unexplored.

Because of this, research has been undertaken into the views of local authority accountants in the north-west on CCT. This paper reports on the findings, building on those reported elsewhere (Wilson, 1999), and focuses on the extent to which CCT, as applied to non-finance white-collar services, had a beneficial impact on service delivery and facilitated a change in attitude amongst local government officers. The findings are placed within a cultural change context, to inform tentative observations concerning Best Value.

CCT AND BV

One aim of CCT was to improve efficiency, and there is evidence, albeit mixed (Boyne, 1998), that this has happened (for example, Walsh, 1991; Walsh and Davies, 1993). However, there has been widespread objection to CCT, not least on the grounds of the transaction costs associated with it and the fact that it has disproportionately affected poorly paid workers and, in particular, females (CPS, 1995). The Labour government's view of CCT is unequivocal: 'In short, CCT has provided a poor deal for employees, employers and local people. CCT will therefore be abolished' (DETR, 1998: 6).

In response to the perceived failings of CCT, Labour has committed itself to the concept of BV, though the precise meaning and nature of it have yet to be determined. However, within the 12 principles that initially defined the BV framework (see DETR, 1998: Fig.1), principle 4 states:

> There is no presumption that services must be privatised, and once the regime is in place there will be no general requirements for councils to put their services out to tender, but there is no reason why services should be delivered directly if other more efficient means are available. What matters is what works.

The pragmatic approach, as shown in principle 4 given above, helps distinguish BV from CCT. It also illustrates that there can be little doubt that Labour is not committed, as a matter of ideology, to in-house provision. The onus is on local authorities to demonstrate that they can achieve the economic objectives of CCT, but without the compulsion and in a manner which is more efficient and customer-focused. To do this, it is necessary that their workforces, both blue- and white-collar, are committed to the pursuit of customer-focused, rather than producer-driven, policies. In many respects this may require a culture shift or a determination to build on the positive aspects of CCT. 'The commitment of local government to the cultural changes which best value is designed to bring about is therefore vital' (DETR, 1998: 7). However, the likelihood of local authority personnel displaying such commitment is open to debate, as also is their ability to do so. Nonetheless, the experience of CCT (combined with the threat of its re-introduction in some form should local authorities fail to respond positively) should mean that the degree of cultural change required successfully to respond to, and to demonstrate, Best Value should be less than would have been necessary had CCT never happened. Whether this is actually the case depends on the impact of CCT.

In an effort to assess the impact of CCT, research has been undertaken into the views of local authority accountants. The importance of finance as a central support service means that accountants constitute a key professional group whose views, attitude and approach will have a major role in the success or otherwise of Best Value.

RESEARCH METHODOLOGY

The objective of the research was to establish the views of qualified accountants on, first, the impact of blue-collar CCT on non-finance white-collar services and, second, the former Conservative government's proposed extension of CCT to those services, that is:

* construction and property services;
* information services;

- legal services;

- personnel services.

Consistent with the results of a survey of finance professionals as reported by Broom (1994), which revealed widespread opposition to CCT, it was hypothesised that accountants in local government in the North West would oppose non-finance white-collar CCT and would do so on the grounds that the process of CCT would lead neither to reduced costs nor improved efficiency nor to improvements in the quality of service delivery.

The north-west was defined, for the purposes of the research, as encompassing 32 local authorities, of which 17 agreed to participate in the questionnaire survey. A detailed breakdown of the region and participating authorities (as at the time of the questionnaire survey, September 1996) is given in Table 1. National figures are also given (note: Table 1 excludes Scottish and Welsh unitary authorities and London boroughs).

TABLE 1

LOCAL GOVERNMENT PROFILE AS AT SEPTEMBER 1996
(EXCLUDING SCOTTISH AND WELSH UNITARIES AND LONDON BOROUGHS)
AND RESEARCH PARTICIPANTS

Regional and National Profile

Political Control	**County Council**		**District Council**		**Metro-politan District**		*Total*	
	NWest	National	NWest	National	NWest	National	NWest	National
Labour	1	7	11	116	14	32	26	*155*
Liberal Democrat	–	3	1	43	–	–	*1*	*46*
Conservative	–	1	–	10	–	–	–	*11*
Independent	–	–	–	11	–	–	–	*11*
No Overall Control	2	24	2	94	1	4	*5*	*122*
Total	3	35	14	274	15	36	32	345

Participating Auths. – Political Control	**County Council**	**District Council**	**Met. District**	*Total*
Labour	1	4	8	*13*
Liberal Democrat				
No Overall Control	1	2	1	*4*
Total	2	6	9	17

Source: Municipal Yearbook 1997

The north-west was chosen as it is professionally and politically representative of the UK. Professionally, the vast majority of qualified accountants in local government are members of the Chartered Institute of Public Finance and Accountancy (CIPFA). Politically, the region is, and was in September 1996 when the research was undertaken, representative of the situation nationally insofar as Labour is by far the dominant party. But there are also four authorities where there is no overall control (see Table 1). In addition, of the Labour authorities, one was traditionally Conservative-controlled up until May 1995 and three others had no overall control until Labour became the ruling party in May 1996; of the authorities with no overall control, in one authority the Conservatives are by far the largest party (with Ratepayers the second largest).

The hypothesis was investigated by means of a questionnaire distributed in September 1996 to 296 professionally qualified accountants employed by the 17 participating local authorities in the north-west region of England. Of the 296 questionnaires, five were returned with a note stating that the person to whom it was addressed had left the authority. The remaining 291 can only be assumed to have found their intended recipients. Of the 291, 164 were returned, a response rate of 56 per cent. All returned questionnaires were correctly completed and could be used. General information on respondents is given in Table 2.

The objective of the questionnaire was to establish the views of finance professionals on CCT and the reasons for them. In doing so, factual information on their background was sought, that is, type and political control of the authority for which they work, type of professional accountancy qualification held, post-qualification experience, previous experience of working in the private sector and seniority (see Table 2). This information was requested in order to examine whether responses are influenced by differences in background.

It can be seen (Table 2) that 77 per cent of respondents are employed in metropolitan authorities and 85 per cent work for authorities which are Labour-controlled, reflecting the fact that 13 of the 17 authorities which participated in the survey were Labour-controlled (Table 1). Eighty-three per cent of respondents are CIPFA qualified, of whom four out of 164 respondents held more than one professional accountancy qualification, but each was CIPFA qualified. For analytical purposes, these have been categorised as non-CIPFA, justified on the basis that those with non-CIPFA qualifications have, by definition, been exposed to a greater level of commercial accountancy practice than someone who is CIPFA qualified only, and this is not negated when dual qualifications are held. Such an exposure to commercial practice could be expected to mean a greater sympathy with the thrust of changes to which local authorities have been subjected.

TABLE 2

GENERAL INFORMATION ON RESPONDENTS

	Number	%
Employing Organisation:		
Metropolitan Authority	126	77
Non-Metropolitan Authority	37	22
No response	1	1
Total	*164*	*100*
Political Control:		
Labour	139	85
Non-Labour	16	10
No response	9	5
Total	*164*	*100*
Accountancy Qualification:		
CIPFA	136	83
Non-CIPFA	27	16
No response	1	1
Total	*164*	*100*
Post-Qualification Experience (Years):		
5 or less	43	26
6-10	24	15
11-15	22	13
16-20	32	19
More than 20	42	26
No response	1	1
Total	*164*	*100*
Experience of Working Full Time in the Private Sector:		
Yes	43	26
No	120	73
No response	1	1
Total	*164*	*100*
Status:		
CFO / DCFO /ACFO/ equivalent	53	32
Non-CFO / DCFO / ACFO equivalent (see below)	108	66
No Response	3	2
Total	*164*	*100*
Non-CFO / DCFO / ACFO equivalent: section worked in:		
Accounting	66	40
Audit	18	11
Other	24	15
Total	*108*	*66*

The responses indicate a good spread of experience, with 26 per cent being qualified for five years or less and 26 per cent being qualified for more than 20 years. The question was based on the assumption that those with most experience could be expected to be less likely to welcome change than those relatively recently qualified. The question helps explore the extent to which accountancy personnel in the north-west were brought up in, and perhaps nostalgic for, a completely different, non-commercial, local authority environment than that which arguably prevails today, that is, an environment in which accountancy practice was unique and only recently has been forced to conform to 'best commercial practice'.

However, post-qualification experience is not simply a matter of chronology. More recently qualified accountants will have undertaken their education and training having studied different subjects and been involved in different work-based tasks. For instance, with regard to professional syllabi, it is not simply a question of different topics being covered under the same subject headings, but actually different subjects now being studied. An example of this is the fact that CIPFA-registered trainees now study business strategy as a discrete, separately examined subject within the context of a specific sector of the trainee's choice (for example, local government, National Health Service). This change was introduced in 1993 and was additional to a fundamental syllabus change in 1990, which was the first change since 1975. These changes reflect the pace of change within the public service environment and the increasing sectoral overlap between public and private sectors. It was assumed that those who had most recently qualified, having been exposed to a more 'private sector' education syllabus, would be more sympathetic to CCT than those who, perhaps, had qualified many years ago and who had been subject to a conventional public sector education and training learning experience.

With regard to experience of working full-time in the private sector, the question is based on the assumption that accountants with private sector experience would be more likely to be supportive of CCT, or at least less antagonistic towards it, and less likely to view it as a threat to job security and established patterns of working. This, it is further assumed, is because they may be used to more flexible working patterns and less likely to regard traditional public sector job security as something which should not be threatened. However, it may also be the case that any movement from private to public sector was for reasons of enhanced job security, possibly at the expense of higher private sector salary levels, and any threat to this could trigger an even greater degree of antagonism to CCT in that it undermines the very reason for the job change.

The questionnaire also asked whether the respondent was a chief financial officer (CFO), deputy CFO (DCFO), assistant CFO (ACFO) or equivalent. Of the respondents, 53 (32 per cent) stated that they were a CFO, DCFO, ACFO or equivalent. Of those who were not, 66 worked in accounting, 18 in audit and 24 in one of the other sections (for example, payroll, creditor payments and so on), representing 40 per cent, 11 per cent and 15 per cent respectively of total respondents. For information, of the 24 working in other sections, nine worked in service departments, one in sundry income collection, one in administration of local taxation, one in treasury management and two in insurance; the remaining ten did not stipulate the section in which they worked.

RESEARCH FINDINGS

In response to the question 'Do you accept the *principle* of *compulsory* competitive tendering for *some or all* non-finance white collar services?', 70 per cent of respondents (115 out of 164) stated they did not. This contrasts with 41 per cent who opposed blue-collar CCT (see Wilson, 1999). Insofar as 30 per cent accept the principle, this again contrasts with the findings reported by Broom (1994) whereby only 16 per cent of respondents were in favour of CCT.

The questionnaire invited those who stated that they accepted the principle of non-finance CCT to indicate the service(s) where CCT should apply. Of the 49 who accepted the principle (30 per cent of respondents), 30 indicated the services they felt should be subject to CCT (see Table 3). Most support was for CCT to be applied to construction and property services, with least support for its application to personnel.

TABLE 3

NON-FINANCE WHITE COLLAR SERVICES: SUPPORT FOR CCT

	Construction & Property Services No.	Information Services No.	Legal Services No.	Personnel Services No.
Support for application of CCT out of 30 responses	28	22	18	15

The significance of the findings needs to be placed within the context of the answer to the question which asked: 'Have you had a direct involvement in white-collar CCT?', to which 59 per cent responded 'YES' and 41 per cent responded 'NO' (the corresponding proportions for blue-collar were 43 per cent and 55 per cent: Wilson, 1999). In other words, it is reasonable to assume that respondents are able to provide informed feedback. Statistical analysis of the responses revealed that there were no significant

TABLE 4

NON-FINANCE WHITE COLLAR CCT:
RELATIONSHIP BETWEEN RESPONDENTS' BACKGROUND AND RESPONSES

Relationship between views on non-finance white collar CCT and:	χ^2 =	p =
Employer	2.15970	0.33965
Political Control	0.02114	0.88439
Accountancy Qualification	1.34221	0.51114
Post-Qualification Experience	2.18415	0.70193
Experience of working in private sector full-time	0.00081	0.97723
Status	0.16977	0.68032

relationships between the background of the respondent (that is, responses as summarised in Table 2 above) and their views on non-finance white-collar CCT (see Table 4).

Respondents were asked to indicate their views on the likely impact of CCT on costs and quality. With regard to cost, respondents were asked to comment on the likely impact of non-finance white-collar CCT on their own organisation's net expenditure. Fifty per cent of respondents believed that net expenditure would be affected, that is, 30 per cent of respondents stated that it would fall and 20 per cent believed it would increase, with 37 per cent believing there would be no effect (11 per cent responded 'Don't Know' and two per cent did not respond). It is interesting to note that there was a significant relationship between responses to this question and those who had previously worked full-time in the private sector (χ^2 = 8.62; p = 0.03). Those with previous private sector experience were more likely than those who had not previously worked in the private sector to say that the process of CCT would have no effect on net expenditure; conversely, those who had not previously worked in the private sector were more likely to say that net expenditure would reduce. This is surprising and does not support the view that those with private sector backgrounds were more likely to see merits in CCT; it may, however, be the case that, insofar as they had any private sector experience or knowledge of competitive tendering in a white-collar context, they had become more sceptical as to its actual impact on expenditure.

Where respondents stated that service costs would be affected by CCT (82 out of 164, that is, 50 per cent as stated above), they were also invited to comment on their views. Comments were provided by four respondents only, but they highlight the importance of taking into account the size of the authority when considering responses to CCT (small-scale volumes of non-finance white-collar activity could only lead, at best, to small-scale savings as a proportion of an authority's overall activity):

> My authority is relatively small, separating client and contractor functions, tender preparation and subsequent monitoring will in my opinion not prove cost-effective in any of [the] services. Most council's [sic] in particular use voluntary private contractors for construction services and many aspects of IT provision.

> Costs may reduce – but if quality deteriorates, customer care suffers and management time wasted.

> Even if tender prices are lower, the costs of monitoring the contract usually outweigh the savings.

> Functions are too small to benefit from cost savings, which outweigh the introduction of a formal client side.

With regard to quality, 48 per cent of respondents believed that quality would be affected, that is, 22 per cent believe that quality would increase and 26 per cent believe it would be reduced, with 39 per cent believing that CCT would have no effect (11 per cent responded 'Don't Know' and two per cent did not respond). Where respondents stated that service quality would be affected by CCT (78 out of 164, that is, 48 per cent), they were also invited to comment on their views, but only five chose to do so and the views are somewhat mixed:

> I think the same overall resources will be used for the service plus the tendering process. This means less time will be spent on the service.

> In all services it should improve even if won in-house as any reorganisation of service should aim to achieve this. This is more likely to be a result of improved management of the service whether int[ernal] or ext[ernal].

> Across services, there will be a reduction [in quality] as providers strive to reduce costs.

> Quality will reduce for all white collar CCT activities if won by the private sector, by use of less qualified staff.

> Within my authority the issue of quality is addressed by the internal market whereby units choose to purchase services, internally or externally – if the quality isn't there then the market demand isn't!

However, 63 per cent and 66 per cent respectively of all respondents stated that it had forced non-finance service managers to place increased emphasis on value for money and to become more customer-oriented (Wilson, 1999) (evidence of the concept of the 'public service orientation', developed in the mid-1980s as a response to the hostile environment confronting local government, see Clarke and Stewart, 1985; 1986; Stewart and Clarke, 1987; Stewart and Ranson, 1988). This is a much greater level of support than that revealed in the survey of (an unspecified number of) chief executives undertaken by the former Department of the Environment (DoE, 1996). Although the survey contained a question which was concerned with all white-collar services as opposed to non-finance white-collar services, 41 per cent believed that the impact of white-collar CCT would be a positive one, while 24 per cent believed it would be negative and 33 per cent stated it would be neutral. The findings are, however, comparable to those of the Local Government Management Board (LGMB, 1997), also based on a survey of chief executives. Based on 143 respondents (who had also responded to earlier surveys in 1992 and 1994), 65 per cent believed competition had reduced the costs of service provision, 71 per cent believed it had increased concern for quality and 69 per cent believed it had increased concern for customer satisfaction.

In order to investigate the extent to which cultural factors may influence views on CCT, a number of related questions were included in the questionnaire (see Wilson, 1999). The objective was to establish whether there is evidence that local authority accountants display a more commercial, less traditional, outlook, consistent with new public management (Hood, 1991; Dunleavy and Hood, 1994) and as recommended by the Audit Commission (1995). The responses reveal that 65 per cent welcome the commercial disciplines imposed by CCT, consistent with the findings of Rao and Young (1995), who, following their study of ten local authorities (six English, two Welsh and two Scottish) state (p.45): 'At least in those authorities visited, the new disciplines which CCT imposed are valued, even where the competition that produced them is not.' However, although 42 per cent (that is, four per cent 'strongly agree' plus 38 per cent 'agree') believe that the same disciplines are welcomed within financial services, 48 per cent (that is, nine per cent 'strongly agree' plus 39 per cent 'agree') do not. This may indicate that individual respondents have a mistaken perception of their colleagues' views on CCT. It may, however, indicate that, within financial services, professional accountants welcome the commercial disciplines but they believe that non-accountants do not. Whatever the explanation, there is some justification in questioning the wider applicability of the findings of Rao and Young (1995).

However, overall the responses indicate a willingness to accept change. This is further illustrated by the overall level of support, 76 per cent (that is, 14 per cent 'strongly agree' plus 62 per cent 'agree'), for the statement that local authorities should adopt a business culture. Although this was recommended by the Audit Commission (1995: 22), the Commission reported that finance departments had failed to embrace the new culture, were insufficiently client-focused, and in fact uncompetitive, with only the cheapest 25 per cent of in-house providers able to match the private sector. The findings, therefore, are surprising but indicate that, on the basis of this survey, accountants would be willing to change their overall approach and adopt private sector practices.

Further statistical analysis revealed that neither previous private sector experience nor type of professional accountancy qualification were significantly related to the belief that local authorities should adopt a business culture. This is interesting in that, for instance, there is no evidence of a difference between those who are CIPFA qualified and those who are not.

However, the findings reveal that finance professionals remain committed to the traditional role of local authorities as direct providers of services, with 88 per cent (that is, 59 per cent 'disagree' plus 29 per cent 'strongly disagree') rejecting the view that the enabling model, the one supported by the former Conservative government, is the most appropriate for local government. Similarly, 83 per cent supported the statement that CCT was introduced for political rather than economic reasons. This perception was always likely to reinforce opposition to CCT. In the case of Best Value, however, a general belief that it is ideologically motivated is unlikely to be evident. The government itself appears keen to avoid such a criticism: 'The Government's approach to improved local services is a pragmatic one. What matters is what works. The form of service delivery should not be determined by ideology' (DETR, 1998: 6).

Overall, the questionnaire survey indicates a willingness to adopt a more commercial approach to financial management. This is also consistent with the findings of Keen and Scase (1998), who, on the basis of an in-depth study of a county council, conclude that 'new managerialism' is no longer rhetoric but the reality of local government officers' employment in the late 1990s. Similarly, Pratchett and Wingfield (1996), on the basis of their research into four local authorities, concluded that there was evidence of a more pro-market outlook and less commitment to the values – collectively constituting a public service ethos (PSE) – which were assumed generally to underpin public service delivery. They also found that the overall attitude and policies of the employing authority had a significant influence on the underlying values of those most exposed to competition (in short, there was less commitment to the concept of PSE in those authorities which had adopted a pro-CCT approach).

CONCLUSION

The key features of the Labour government's policy towards local government, as announced in the Queen's Speech November 1998, indicate that the emphasis, within Best Value, will be on setting and monitoring performance. New audit and inspection arrangements are to be introduced, with 'hit squads' to be sent in to councils deemed to be failing. Conversely, high performers will become 'beacon' councils and will be regarded as centres of excellence. They may also enjoy greater financial autonomy. In short, rewards for 'success' and penalties for 'failure' are likely to be significant.

Labour appears to assume, however, that the incidence of 'failure' may be expected to be high unless considerable improvement occurs in the management of local authorities. Hilary Armstrong, local government minister, has stated: '*Nothing less than a fundamental change in political culture is needed* ... Councils will be required to consult on how they deliver Best Value services. This will give power to the citizen and make councils more customer-oriented, *delivering services in the interests of the user rather than the provider*' (Armstrong, 1998: 20–21 – emphasis added). It is significant that, after 18 years of Conservative government and ten years after the introduction of CCT, Labour believes that a 'fundamental change' in culture is still required and appears to believe that service delivery is producer- rather than customer-driven. If this is an accurate diagnosis, it leads to obvious doubts as to the extent to which Labour, adopting an approach less dogmatic than that of the Conservatives, will be successful in bringing about change.

However, Labour's commitment to abolish CCT may itself increase the chances of achieving improvements in service delivery, reflecting, as it does, an increased awareness of the demerits of adversarial competition (Milne, 1997). Absence of trust, lack of co-operation, short-termism, transaction costs and bureaucracy are all identified as being associated with contracting and contrast with the possible merits, for private and public sectors, of partnership and trust. Organisational relationships may be contractually based, but the nature of the relationship should be trustful, co-operative and long term rather than distrustful, adversarial and short term. In other words, increased emphasis is likely to be placed on collaboration, not least between public and private sectors, in service delivery. However, Labour still sees merit in competition, which 'will continue to be an essential management tool for securing improvement, and an important means of demonstrating in a transparent way that best value is being obtained' (DETR, 1998: 20). Though it is also recognised that competition 'is not in itself enough to demonstrate that Best Value is being achieved' (DETR, 1998: Fig.1, principle 5).

Whether local government is capable of capitalising on the new environment created by Labour has yet to be proved. However, on the basis of the findings reported here, though there was opposition amongst finance professionals to non-finance white-collar CCT, the opposition was mainly based on the issue of quality rather than costs. In addition, there is recognition of clear benefits of CCT. More fundamentally, there is evidence of a willingness to undergo cultural change in the provision of services. Given the predominance of Labour-controlled councils in the north-west, perhaps even stronger evidence may be revealed if the views of finance professionals were investigated in those authorities which are not Labour-controlled (see Practhett and Wingfield, 1996). Whether such evidence would have been found had CCT never happened is open to debate, but the existence and experience of CCT has, it seems reasonable to conclude, placed authorities in a better position than they would otherwise have been in to respond to Best Value.

REFERENCES

Armstrong, H., 1998, 'Modernisation on the Menu', *Public Finance*, 27 Nov., pp.20–23.

Audit Commission, 1995, *From Administration to Management: The Management of the Finance Function in Local Government* (London: HMSO).

Blair, A., 1998, *Leading the Way: A New Vision for Local Government* (London: Institute of Public Policy Research).

Boyne, G., 1998, 'Competitive Tendering in Local Government: A Review of Theory and Evidence', *Public Administration*, Vol.76, No.4, pp.695–712.

Broom, D., 1994, 'Pragmatists all in the Shadow of Competition', *Public Finance*, 2 Sept., pp.10–12.

Clarke, M. and J. Stewart, 1985, *Local Government and the Public Service Orientation: Or Does a Public Service Provide for the Public?* (London: Local Government Training Board).

Clarke, M. and J. Stewart, 1986, *The Public Service Orientation – Developing the Approach* (London: Local Government Training Board).

CPS (Centre for Public Services), 1995, *The Gender Impact of CCT in Local Government: Calculation of the National Costs and Savings of CCT* (Sheffield: CPS).

DETR (Department of the Environment, Transport and the Regions), 1998, *Modernising Local Government: Improving Local Services through Best Value* (London: DETR).

DoE (Department of the Environment), 1996, *Competition News*, No.5, Jan.–March (London: DoE).

Dunleavy, P. and C. Hood, 1994, 'From Old Public Administration to New Public Management', *Public Money and Management*, Vol.14, No.3, pp.9–16.

Harding, D., 1998, 'The Late Converts', *Public Finance*, 27 Feb., pp.12–13.

Hood, C., 1991, 'A Public Management for all Seasons?', *Public Administration*, Vol.69, No.1, pp.3–19.

Keen, L. and R. Scase, 1998, *Local Government Management: The Rhetoric and Reality of Change* (Buckingham: Open University Press).

Local Government Management Board (LGMB), 1997, *Portrait of Change 1997* (Luton: LGMB).

Milne, S., 1997, *Report on Contracts and Competition Programme: Making Markets Work* (London: University of London).

Pratchett, L. and Wingfield, M., 1996, 'Petty Bureaucracy and Woolly-Minded Liberalism? The Changing Ethos of Local Government Officers', *Public Administration*, Vol.74, pp.639–56.

Rao, N. and K. Young, 1995, *Competition, Contracts And Change: The Local Authority Experience of CCT* (London: LGC Communications).

Stewart, J. and M. Clarke, 1987, 'The Public Service Orientation: Issues and Dilemmas', *Public Administration*, Vol.65, pp.161–78.

Stewart, J. and S. Ranson, 1988, 'Management in the Public Domain', *Public Money and Management*, Vol.8, No.2, pp.11–18.

Walsh, K., 1991, *Competitive Tendering for Local Authority Services: Initial Experiences* (London: HMSO).

Walsh, K. and H. Davis, 1993, *Competition and Service: The Impact of the Local Government Act 1988* (London: HMSO).

Wilson, J., 1999, 'Compulsory Competitive Tendering and Local Government Financial Services: An Analysis of the Views of Local Government Accountants in the North West of England', *Public Administration* (forthcoming).

Picking Winners or Piloting Best Value?
An Analysis of English Best Value Bids

STEVE MARTIN

The Best Value pilot programme established in England by the Department of the Environment, Transport and the Regions represents an attempt to develop a new style of policy making which relies more on persuasion and less on detailed prescription and regulation than the Compulsory Competitive Tendering regime introduced under the Conservative governments of the 1980s and early 1990s. The programme includes a range of different types of local authority, as well as two police forces. It spans all major local authority services and functions and embraces a wide variety of approaches to achieving Best Value. This heterogeneity makes evaluating the impacts of Best Value on service costs and standards difficult. However, it increases the chances of securing broad based support for the Best Value regime and stimulating organisational and cultural change in local government.

In the late summer of 1997 local authorities and police forces in England were invited by the Department of the Environment, Transport and the Regions (DETR) to bid to take part in a programme designed to pilot Best Value. Unlike bids to the various 'challenge initiatives' introduced over the last ten years, authorities were competing not for additional funding but for the chance to play a role in shaping the framework which will replace Compulsory Competitive Tendering (CCT). Briefings given by key government advisers made it clear that the 'stakes were high'. The consequences of a failure to modernise council services through Best Value would, we were told, 'not be more CCT but less local government'. Local authorities were, in effect, being offered a 'deal', at first outlined in private by the Prime Minister to leading local politicians and then later spelt out publicly in his address to the Labour Local Government Conference in February 1998 and subsequent pamphlet (IPPR 1998). Councils that are able to re-invigorate local democracy in their areas, deliver good local

Steve Martin, University of Warwick

services 'at an acceptable price' and maintain high standards of conduct will, he promised, be rewarded with greater autonomy and perhaps increased funding. Those which fail to do so will have resources and responsibilities for delivering local services taken away from them.

Senior local politicians and local authority officers responded with enthusiasm to the invitation to participate in the Best Value pilot programme, with more than a third of councils submitting bids (Filkin and Corrigan, 1997). Their proposals were appraised by an 'Evaluation Panel' comprising DETR officials and senior representatives from the Confederation of British Industry's Procurement Panel, two trades unions, the Audit Commission, the Local Government Association and the Government Office for the Eastern Region. In December 1997 the Local Government Minister announced that she had accepted in full the panel's recommendation that 37 pilot initiatives, involving 40 local authorities and two police forces,[1] be included in a two-year pilot programme starting the following April. The 'pilots' were offered exemption from 1988 CCT legislation (but not the provisions of the 1980 Local Government and Planning Act) and a further 16 councils which had submitted bids were invited to apply for selective exemptions to enable them to take forward their proposals outside of the pilot programme.[2]

The remainder of this paper analyses the 155 Best Value bids and, in particular, the characteristics of those which were selected as pilot projects, in order to assess the role which the pilot programme is likely to play in the development and implementation of the Best Value regime.

THE BIDDERS

Neither the local authorities which bid to participate in the pilot programme nor the 40 councils involved in the successful bids are a statistically representative sample of English local government as a whole. Two-thirds of all metropolitan districts, just over half of all unitaries and London boroughs and almost 50 per cent of shire counties submitted bids, compared to just one in four shire district councils (Table 1). A significantly higher proportion of the bids submitted by unitaries and London boroughs were included in the programme than was the case for other categories of authorities, whereas relatively few bids submitted by shire districts were accepted. As a result, and because a lower percentage of shire districts than any other kind of authority submitted bids, less than five per cent of all English shire districts are represented in the pilot programme.

Similarly, neither the bids nor the pilot projects were distributed evenly across the country. London boroughs feature prominently in the programme (half submitted bids and 20 per cent were selected for inclusion) as do

TABLE 1

TYPE OF AUTHORITY

Type of authority	% submitted bids	% selected as pilots	% bids selected as pilots	% pilot programme
Metropolitan districts	67	19	29	18
Unitaries	55	26	46	18
Shire counties	49	15	29	13
London boroughs	50	19	37	16
Shire districts	27	4	14	26
Police	12	5	33	5
Mixed[1]			25	3

Note: [1] Includes four bids involving collaboration between authorities from different tiers (one of which was selected for inclusion in the pilot programme) and bids submitted by a housing association and the districts surveyors.

authorities from the north (although fewer than 40 per cent submitted bids, a higher proportion of bidders were selected than was the case in any other region). At the other end of the spectrum, authorities from the south-west and east midlands regions were least inclined to submit proposals and comprise a relatively small proportion of those included in the pilot programme. The west midlands is also underrepresented. This is not, however, the result of a lack of bids but because only two of the bids submitted by councils from the region were successful (though it is better represented than other regions among the 16 authorities offered selective exemptions from CCT).

The vast majority (90 per cent) of bids were submitted by single authorities. Similarly, there are only two joint pilots – the 'CWOIL' initiative, which is focusing on housing and related services in Cambridge, Welwyn, Oxford, Ipswich and Lincoln, and a project being undertaken by Brighton and Hove, Tandridge and Wealden to explore the potential for the joint delivery of revenue services. Thirty (75 per cent) of the local authorities involved in the pilots were Labour-controlled, seven were under no overall control, three were Conservative and there was one Liberal Democrat authority. This reflects the dominant position of Labour in local government at the time but, underrepresents councils controlled by the Liberal Democrats.

Members of the Evaluation Panel represented a range of different interests and sought to ensure that the pilot programme reflected approaches that they considered to be important. Both business representatives and the DETR stressed the need for the programme to include initiatives that would use competition as a means of checking the cost-effectiveness of services. The trades union representatives were particularly supportive of bids that

TABLE 2

REGIONAL DISTRIBUTION OF BIDDERS AND PILOTS

Type of authority	% of authorities bidders	from region pilots	% bids selected pilots
Eastern	43	9	22
East Midlands	26	6	25
London	50	19	37
Merseyside	40	0	0
North East	38	15	40
North West	39	10	25
South East	45	10	23
South West	34	7	20
West Midlands	45	5	11
Yorkshire & Humberside	43	15	33

stressed the importance of staff involvement in Best Value initiatives. The Audit Commission fed into the process external auditors' analyses of the bids, and the two panel members from local government backgrounds emphasised the importance of allowing authorities freedom to experiment with alternative approaches to Best Value. However, party political considerations seemed not to be a determining factor. Instead, the formal selection process was marked by a high degree of consensus in which the prime concern on all sides seemed to be to agree a programme of initiatives that, taken as a whole, were likely to reflect and test out the broad thrust of the Best Value principles.

In making its choices the Evaluation Panel drew upon summaries of each bid and a database listing their key characteristics in relation to the Best Value principles outlined by the DETR. The summaries described the proposals contained in each bid using a standard template which covered the key issues that authorities were asked to address in their proposals, that is, community involvement, performance measurement/ management, service review, the use of competition, quality assurance and management, sharing information with other authorities, selecting activities/services for inclusion in the pilot, assessment of the costs and risks associated with their proposals, and details of the level of support which the proposed pilot enjoyed within and beyond the authority. In addition the panel asked that the summaries gave details of any proposals outlined in the bids for involving front-line staff in the proposed initiatives.

The database covered similar issues to the summaries but gave more details of the focus of each bid, the authorities' assessment of their current performance in the areas in which it was proposed to pilot Best Value, the range of these activities (CCT and non-CCT, regulatory, statutory, enabling services), the range of providers which were to be involved in the pilot (in-house, other public agencies, voluntary sector, private sector), the ways in which competition would be used, the nature of proposals for innovative forms of service delivery, the mechanisms proposed for undertaking reviews, whether a community plan had been prepared or was being developed, the level of input to the proposals from service users, the level of internal and external support for the bid, evidence of clear proposals for disseminating the lessons of the pilot to the community and to other authorities, evidence from the bid of the authority's capacity to carry through major organisational changes, and an analysis of the value which the pilot would add to the programme as a whole.

THE BIDS

Under the Best Value framework, outlined in the 12 'Best Value principles' issued in July 1997 (DETR, 1997) and developed in a consultation paper issued in March 1998 (DETR, 1998), it is expected that authorities will review all of their services over a five-year period. However, only a quarter of the authorities which bid to pilot Best Value envisaged applying it to all of their services during the next five years. Most of these 'whole authority' bids planned to focus on services which accounted for a total of 40–50 per cent of their budget during the two-year pilot period but were also committed to reviewing all other services in the following three years. Similarly, a quarter of the pilots (Braintree District Council, Brighton and Hove Council, Bristol City Council, Ipswich Borough Council, Lincolnshire County Council, London Borough of Camden, London Borough of Lewisham, London Borough of Newham, Redcar and Cleveland Borough Council and Warwickshire County Council) plan to apply Best Value to all services within the next four to five years. (A number of others, for example Greater Manchester Police, plan to apply it to all services but in only part of the areas they serve.)

The Best Value principles and the consultation paper state that councils should start by reviewing those services that are seen as being the 'weakest'. The White Paper (Cm 4014, 1998) and draft Local Government Bill (House of Commons, 1998a) acknowledge the importance of a number of other considerations in determining the timing of reviews but retain a presumption that councils will wish to tackle their weaker services early on. However, the bids suggested a wide variety of other rationales for the choice of services and a significant proportion explicitly rejected the so-called 'worst first' criterion favoured by ministers. Some did so because they believed that it was better to pilot Best Value in areas where they could be confident of achieving 'early gains' (for example, by externalising services to achieve efficiency gains or through the development of joint ventures which released additional capital investment in services). Others were concerned about the impact on staff morale of stigmatising weaker services or because they believed their authorities lacked the capacity to deal with all of the worst performing services at the same time. A third group argued that it was important to focus in the early stages on services which were seen as vital to the achievement of their corporate vision and/or those which were known to be of particular concern to local residents.

Authorities that did follow the government's guidance defined poorly performing services in a variety of different ways. Some used CCPIs, others focused on user feedback or residents' surveys and others saw benchmarking as the best way of highlighting services which needed urgent attention. A number focused on activities which were known to be relatively costly, whilst others were more concerned with services where standards were seen as relatively low. Many used a combination of several of these criteria.

The bids also reflected a variety of different definitions of what constitutes a 'service'. In line with recent attempts by many authorities to provide more 'holistic government' (see Perri 6, 1997), a significant proportion of authorities rejected a service-based approach, arguing that Best Value can only really be achieved by integrating activities in ways which cut across traditional departmental and committee responsibilities. Some proposed to integrate services targeted on particular client groups, for example, the elderly (Southampton), users with learning disabilities (Cumbria), or young people (Sunderland).

Just under a fifth of the bids, and a quarter of those selected as pilots, adopted a geographical focus. Many of these proposed integrating some or all services within particular wards or localities. The size of these target areas varied considerably. Exeter's pilot projects, for example, are focused on a third of the city, Greater Manchester Police is applying Best Value to all its activities in four of its 25 sub-districts, Leeds City Council is piloting Best Value across 12 services in just two wards, Manchester City Council is exploring three broad activities (improvements in physical appearance, increases in levels of educational attainment and reductions in nuisance and crime) in three areas and Brent is concentrating on just one service (housing) in one part of the borough (Kilburn). A third group of bids focused on so-called 'wicked issues'. Examples from among those chosen as pilots include Bradford MBC (community safety), South Norfolk Council (social exclusion) and Portsmouth City Council (regeneration).

Between them the pilot initiatives span the whole range of local authority functions (Table 3). They also encompass the complete spectrum of council activities and services and all but one of the pilots covers both 'CCT services' and those not subject to CCT legislation. The vast majority (almost 90 per cent) are applying Best Value to statutory, regulatory and enabling services. More than three-quarters of the bids and 95 per cent of the pilots included both front-line and support services. Only one pilot is focusing exclusively on corporate services and just two are concerned exclusively with front-line services.

TABLE 3

ACTIVITIES COVERED BY PILOTS

Service/activity	Number of pilots
Regulatory services	2
Corporate processes	4
Transport	4
Central support functions	4
Leisure	8
Revenues and Benefits	8
Education	8
Direct services	10
Social Services	14
Housing	15

Note: Whole authority pilots will, by definition, apply Best Value principles to all services and are not therefore included in this table.

Some activities feature particularly prominently in the pilot programme, whilst a number are clearly underrepresented. In particular, large proportions of the pilots are applying Best Value to housing management, benefits and/or revenues, services to elderly people, corporate services (such as IT, personnel, payroll, finance and legal services), environmental services (such as refuse collection, street cleansing and waste management) and leisure and cultural services (including in particular library services and the management of sports and leisure centres). By contrast, although a number are piloting Best Value in areas such as adult education, early years provision, school meals and youth and community services, relatively few authorities are focusing on the administration of LEAs or levels of attainment in schools.

The Best Value principles (like the subsequent Consultation Paper, White Paper and draft Local Government Bill) made it clear that the Best Value framework requires that service users, local residents and local businesses become more closely involved in setting and monitoring services standards and costs. It is therefore no surprise that almost all (93 per cent) of the bids, and all of those selected as pilots, outlined proposals for involving users, and that all but one of the pilots, and 85 per cent of the bids, outlined clear proposals for disseminating the results of the proposed initiatives to them. Similarly, a large proportion of both the bidders and pilots (80 per cent and 86 per cent respectively) proposed involving not just users but also representatives of the wider community and most planned to involve the private and voluntary sectors in service reviews.

Fewer than half (42 per cent) of bidders but 66 per cent of those selected as pilots claimed that users and/or the community had been involved in the formulation of their bid, either through direct consultations or, more often, by using existing user feedback to inform the selection of services to be included in the pilot. The pilots also typically claimed a broader base of support for their proposals than the other authorities which submitted bids (see Table 4) and expressed a greater level of commitment to the involvement of external stakeholders. In particular, they were far more likely to envisage a role for the voluntary sector in service reviews (see Table 5). The pilots were also noticeably more committed to sharing the lessons which emerged from their pilots than were other authorities. Almost three-quarters outlined clear proposals for exchanging information with other pilots (compared to just over half of the bidders as a whole) and 81 per cent had plans to network with authorities outside of the pilot programme (compared to 56 per cent of bidders as a whole).

Consulting users and residents about local services and priorities is another key element of the Best Value framework. The proposals put forward in the bids spanned the full range of existing approaches identified

TABLE 4

SUPPORT FOR PROPOSALS

Stakeholder	% bids	% pilots
Council Leader(s)	61	61
Leaders of other groups	48	55
Chief Executive/senior management	60	68
Trades Unions	28	40
Auditor	22	31
Business	19	32
Community groups	17	29
Other	17	32

TABLE 5

STAKEHOLDER INVOLVEMENT IN SERVICE REVIEWS

	% bids	% pilots
Community	81	86
Business	72	82
Voluntary sector	50	74
Other	15	16

by Stoker (1997), including formal consultation, involvement in establishing service-level agreements, area and interest-based forums, broader 'visioning' exercises and attempts to engage with and empower disadvantaged or marginalised groups. The techniques by which bidders proposed to improve engagement with the public were also largely familiar ones. They included:

- the provision of higher quality information via freephone lines, information points, roadshows and community access to information technology;

- the development of improved systems for handling enquiries including for example the establishing of 'one stop shops' and call centres;

- a variety of approaches to gathering information about the users' and residents' perceptions and priorities including surveys, needs analyses, panels, community meetings, 'mystery users', citizens' panels and area, issue or client based forums;

- a range of mechanisms designed to promote deliberative democracy including the development of stronger links with parish councils and the establishment of citizens' juries and citizens' polls.

Very few authorities had no prior experience of any of these approaches. Typically, though, they saw the Best Value framework as requiring them to develop their existing practices in four main ways. First, by transferring expertise from departments which were seen as having effective consultative mechanisms to those which did not. Second, by broadening the range of stakeholders which they consulted to include not only users but also non-users, different communities of interest, the business sector and, in some cases, visitors and/or commuters. Third, by developing a more co-ordinated approach across the whole authority in order to make better use of the information gained from consultation. Fourth, by finding ways of involving stakeholders in designing and specifying future service standards and methods of delivery, rather than simply consulting them about past performance.

Possibly because it was not one of the key criteria listed in the Best Value principles which authorities were asked to address in their bids, few outlined specific plans for informing staff about Best Value initiatives and/or involving them in the selection of areas for review. Nevertheless, in spite of the lack of detailed proposals, just over 40 per cent of bids, and a similar proportion of those selected as pilots, referred to the importance of staff development and involvement and some authorities intended to include trades union representatives on Best Value committees and steering groups.

The 12 'Best Value principles' and the Consultation Paper emphasised central government's view that competition is 'an essential management tool for securing improvement, and an important means of demonstrating in a transparent way that best value is being obtained' (DETR, 1998). Authorities are therefore expected to subject services to market testing except in cases where they 'are able to argue convincingly why this is inappropriate' (DETR, 1998). However, voluntary competitive tendering was mentioned by only 61 per cent of bidders and 66 per cent of those selected as pilots, and there is evidence that even in these authorities it does not enjoy the wholehearted support of backbench members. Similarly, whilst the trades unions have supported the Best Value framework at national level, some local branches have been hostile to pilot projects which stress the externalisation of services, and both the TUC and the CBI have also expressed doubts about the use of market testing as a means of comparing the effectiveness of in-house and external providers (House of Commons, 1998b). Many of the bidders expected benchmarking to play at least as important a role in ensuring service quality and cost effectiveness as market testing. Many proposed to use existing benchmarking groups such as the 'Core Cities Group', the Inter-Authority Group, regional branches of the Policy Performance Research Network and 'audit families'.

The Consultation Paper also advocated the creation of a 'more healthy and diverse market for local services' involving other agencies in service reviews and the development of partnerships between authorities and the private and voluntary sectors to enable joint delivery of local services (DETR, 1998). Almost three-quarters of the bids and 79 per cent of those selected as pilots proposed the development of new joint ventures with the private sector and just over half (56 per cent) of bids and 71 per cent of those selected as pilots anticipated entering into new partnerships with the voluntary sector. These proposals included a wide range of different models of partnership and approaches to procurement. At a strategic level, some authorities planned to establish multi-agency steering or advisory groups to oversee their pilot projects. Others emphasised the role of community partnerships and/or the not-for-profit sector. Many emphasised the need for closer joint working with the police, health authorities and a range of other public sector agencies. A number of bids outlined plans to develop joint service delivery with neighbouring authorities and/or between counties and districts. Many authorities expressed a desire to establish new forms of longer term and less conflict-ridden contracting with the private sector.

According to the consultation paper the process of service review is 'designed to ensure that demanding targets for efficiency and quality improvement are set' and to test that authorities are managing to achieve 'the underlying objective' of maintaining sustained, year on year improvements (DETR, 1998). Another key requirement of the Best Value framework is therefore that authorities establish benchmarks and targets which enable local people, auditors and inspectors to evaluate their performance. Central government has stipulated that baselines will be an integral part of the local performance plans produced by each council. Nearly all of the authorities which submitted bids saw the development of performance targets, local performance indicators and the increased use of benchmarking as important to their proposed initiatives. All but three of the pilots and 80 per cent of bidders planned to develop additional, measurable targets for all piloted services, though few bids contained detailed proposals for achieving this. Three-quarters of the bidders and 90 per cent of pilots expected to involve local users in developing the local performance indicators for at least some services. Only five per cent of bidders, and the same proportion of pilots, committed themselves to user involvement in establishing indicators for all of the services in which they were planning to pilot Best Value.

Just over half of the authorities which submitted bids had secured external 'quality' accreditation. Almost three-quarters were pursuing or already held ISO 9000 accreditation, two-thirds had introduced quality circles, 64 per cent were either working towards or had been awarded Investors in People and just under a third had gained Chartermarks. There was considerable interest among the bidders, and a number of the pilots, in using the Business Excellence Model as a framework within which to pilot Best Value.

THE PURPOSE OF PILOTING

In formal terms, the bidding process and pilot programme can be seen as having two main objectives. First, central government wishes to be able to assess the likely impact on service quality and costs of applying the Best Value framework to all local authorities. Second, both central and local government see the piloting process as offering an opportunity to test out 'what works' and to disseminate 'good practice' to other local authorities. A third, less explicit but equally important, objective has been to build a broad base of support for the Best Value framework among key stakeholders at national and local level and to encourage local authorities and police forces to press ahead with its implementation in advance of legislation.

These three objectives are not mutually exclusive. However, they are probably not equally well served by the approach that has been taken to piloting Best Value. An accurate assessment of the likely outcomes of a universal Best Value framework requires the impacts of all the pilot projects to be aggregated and then 'factored up'. This kind of analysis would be easiest if the pilots were a representative sample of English local councils and police authorities were piloting Best Value in a representative sample of services, were adopting similar approaches to Best Value, seeking similar results and had a common approach to outcome measurement. It would also suggest the need for a pilot programme of sufficient duration to allow evaluation of outcomes over the medium term.

By contrast, highlighting best practice and encouraging other authorities to emulate it is probably best served by selecting as pilots those authorities which are at the leading edge of current practice (and therefore able to offer valuable insights to other councils) and by an evaluation which seeks to identify successful processes (rather than outcomes) and is able to provide rapid feedback to the policy makers and practitioners charged with developing the Best Value framework. In short, the focus is likely to be less on the '3 Es' (economy, efficiency and effectiveness) than on '3Ds' – *developing* new approaches, *demonstrating* their success and *disseminating* 'good practice'.

Our analysis of the characteristics of the pilots suggests that the programme fits the second of these two models rather better than the first. It is clear that neither the bidders nor the pilots are a representative sample of English local government. Different regions and different tiers are not equally represented. More importantly, by virtue of the fact that they wished to participate in the programme, authorities that submitted bids can reasonably be assumed to be among the most supportive of the Best Value principles and the pilots have tended to embrace the Best Value framework more wholeheartedly than other bidders. They might therefore be expected to make more rapid progress in implementing it than would a representative sample of authorities. In particular, most of the 11 'whole authority' pilots which are attempting to review the volume of activities that all authorities will eventually be required to provide each year have unusually robust service review and performance planning systems. As a result, their capacity to sustain the volume and quality of fundamental performance reviews being sought by ministers may not be an accurate guide to what most other councils will actually be able to achieve. Similarly, since some services feature more prominently than others in the pilot initiatives it is unclear whether the challenges involved in implementing Best Value, and the benefits of doing so, will be accurately reflected in the programme. Moreover, the outcomes of the range of very different approaches to Best Value (service-based, area-focused, thematic and so forth) will not be easy to aggregate and it is unlikely that all of the outcomes of the pilot initiatives will be apparent before the legislation and statutory guidance are finalised.

This does not imply that the process by which the pilots were selected was flawed or that summative evaluation of impacts on the pilot services is impossible. However, it does suggest that the pilot programme reflects a number of different political and policy imperatives. These include the desire of the new Labour government to move towards the replacement of CCT in advance of new primary legislation. Ministers have also wanted to demonstrate that Best Value will not be a 'soft option' and that, as in other sectors (including for example the health service and education), greater local autonomy will have to be earned by demonstrating both a willingness and a capacity to 'modernise'. Thirdly, the programme has signalled a commitment to a more inclusive style of policy making in which the business community, trades unions and local government all have a role in working with central government to shape legislation. The bidding process gave local councils and a range of other stakeholders an opportunity to influence the development of Best Value at an early stage. The importance placed by many authorities on the need to achieve more integrated service delivery was, for example, reflected in the subsequent Consultation Paper, which emphasised the need for 'joined up' approaches to Best Value. Similarly, the involvement of the trades unions and others in the selection process meant that, in contrast to the 12 Best Value principles, which failed to mention the role of employees, the Consultation Paper stressed that it is vital that staff are 'involved in any plans to change the way in which services are provided, and are consulted about changes in service conditions or employment terms' (DETR, 1998). As it has evolved, the pilot programme has offered the pilots further opportunities to influence the policy processes both through formal evaluation processes and through informal meetings and contacts with ministers and officials.

The selection of the pilot projects seems, then, to represent a compromise between the need to facilitate the development and dissemination of effective approaches to Best Value, the desire to win support for the framework and the requirement to measure its impacts on the quality and cost of local services. The developmental emphasis accounts for the selection of a number of authorities which appear to be particularly well equipped to implement the Best Value framework. It also explains the inclusion of a wide range of different approaches to achieving Best Value and the selection of authorities which expressed a strong commitment to sharing the information and experience gained from their pilots. However, unlike the 'challenge initiatives' introduced by the previous administration, the outcome of the 'competition' to pilot Best Value was never intended to lead to the winners taking all. Instead the aim has been to create a cadre of 'trail blazing' authorities for others to follow. This reflects a new style of central government policy making which relies in the first instance on persuasion rather than legislation (whilst also retaining the option, in the medium term, to punish councils that fail to modernise). The early signs are that this approach has been successful in encouraging the adoption of Best

Value principles in a wide range of authorities. Two in five local councils bid to be part of the pilot programme – twice as many as ministers and their officials had expected. As a result the pilot programme includes significantly more authorities than had originally been planned (and is much larger than is needed to test out the framework). Moreover, many of the councils that submitted bids but were not included in the programme have decided to proceed with some or all of their proposals, and a recent study suggests that a majority of authorities which did not submit bids also intend to apply Best Value to some or all of their activities in advance of legislation (Martin *et al.*, 1998).

The extent to which this momentum for change can be sustained in the longer term will depend crucially on the development of more effective channels for exchange of experience between local government, central government and other sectors. It will also be conditioned by the ability of the participants in this experiment to reconcile the different demands of assessing outcomes, learning lessons and generating support for and ownership of the policy. Whether they are able to strike an appropriate balance between these multiple objectives will determine the chances of developing a framework which, rather than being imposed from the centre and resisted at local level, will facilitate the delivery of better local services and in so doing may help to encourage long term changes in the culture and organisation of English local government.

NOTES

1. Thirty-three 'single authority' bids were selected for inclusion – Birmingham City Council, Bradford Metropolitan District Council, Braintree District Council, Bristol City Council, Carrick District Council, City of York, Cumbria County Council, Exeter City Council, Gosport Borough Council, Great Yarmouth Borough Council, Ipswich Borough Council, Leeds City Council, Lincolnshire County Council, London Borough of Brent, London Borough of Camden, London Borough of Greenwich, London Borough of Harrow, London Borough of Lewisham, London Borough of Newham, Manchester City Council, Newark and Sherwood District Council, Newcastle upon Tyne Metropolitan Borough Council, Northamptonshire County Council, Oldham Metropolitan Borough Council, Portsmouth City Council, Reading Borough Council, Redcar and Cleveland Borough Council, South Norfolk Council, Southampton City Council, City of Sunderland, Surrey County Council, Warwickshire County Council, Watford Council Borough Council. In addition, two joint bids from Brighton and Hove, Tandridge District Council and Wealden Borough Council, and the City of Lincoln, Cambridge City Council, Welwyn Borough Council, Oxford City Council and Ipswich Borough Council were selected, as were the proposals submitted by the Cleveland Police Authority and Greater Manchester Police. At the DETR's request the independent evaluation of the pilot programme has also included the 'whole authority bid' submitted by Brighton and Hove Council.
2. The 16 'co-pilots' are Bedford Borough Council, Cambridge City Council, Coventry City Council, Crawley Borough Council, Durham County Council, East Hertfordshire District Council, Epsom & Ewell Borough Council, King's Lynn & West Norfolk Borough Council, Kirklees Metropolitan Borough Council, Leicester City Council, London Borough of

Southwark, Middlesborough Council, Sheffield City Council, Solihull Metropolitan Borough Council, Walsall Metropolitan Borough Council and Wolverhampton Metropolitan Borough Council.

3. The author is a member of the research team commissioned by the Department of the Environment, Transport and the Regions to monitor and evaluate the Best Value pilot programme. The views expressed are his own and do not necessarily represent those of the Department.

REFERENCES

Audit Commission, 1998, 'Learning from the Pilots' (unpublished paper to the Best Value Advisory Group).

Cm 4014, 1998, 'Modern Local Government: In Touch with the People' (London: HMSO).

House of Commons, 1998a, *Local Government Bill*, 52/2 (London: House of Commons).

House of Commons, 1998b, *Implementation of the Best Value framework: Minutes of Evidence to the Environment, Transport and Regional Affairs Committee: Eleventh Report Vol. 1* (London: HMSO).

DETR, 1997, *The Twelve Principles of Best Value* (London: DETR).

DETR, 1998a, *Modernising Local Government: Improving Local Services through Best Value* (DETR, London).

Filkin, G. and P. Corrigan, 1997, *Learning from the Bids* (London: Local Government Management Board).

Martin, S.J. *et al.*, 1998, *Best Value: Current Developments and Challenges* (London: LGA).

IPPR, 1998, *Leading the Way: A New Vision for Local Government* (London: IPPR).

Labour Party, 1997, *Britain Deserves Better* (London: Labour Party).

Perri 6, 1997, *Holistic Government* (London: Demos).

Stoker, G., 1997, 'Local Political Participation', in *New Perspectives on Local Governance* (York: Joseph Rowntree Foundation).

Best Value in Welsh Local Government: Progress and Prospects

GEORGE A. BOYNE, JULIAN GOULD-WILLIAMS, JENNIFER LAW and RICHARD WALKER

The development and distinctive characteristics of Best Value in Wales are analysed on the basis of an extensive set of interviews with elected members and officers in all of the Welsh pilot authorities. The close relationship between the Welsh Office and the Welsh Local Government Association has shaped the Best Value regime. These organisations have steered the formulation of the policy, and have drivem its implementation at a faster pace than in England. A consequence is that Welsh pilots have confronted difficult issues concerning performance plans and service reviews ahead of their English counterparts. The prospects for the implementation of Best Value are evaluated on the basis of Welsh pilots' experience with the first wave of 127 service reviews.

BEST VALUE IN WELSH LOCAL GOVERNMENT: PROGRESS AND
PROSPECTS

Local government in Wales has conventionally been regarded as simply a sub-division of that in England. Historically, Welsh local government has had largely the same structure, functions and processes as its English counterpart. However, over the last 30 years, a more distinctive and separate system of local government has emerged. This trend can be traced back to the creation of the Welsh Office in 1965, and the subsequent growth of Welsh policy networks in areas such as housing and education (Boyne *et al.*, 1991; Farrell and Law, 1998). Although the Welsh Office remains responsible for the implementation of policies that emanate from Westminster and Whitehall, it has become less unusual for such policies to be modified to suit circumstances in Wales. The most marked recent expression of this 'Welsh effect' is in the structure of local government. Whereas England has a mixture of two-tier and single-tier systems, the

George Boyne, Julian Gould-Williams and Richard Walker, Cardiff University; Jennifer Law, University of Glamorgan structure throughout Wales consists of 22 unitary authorities (Boyne, 1997b). Moreover, the establishment of the Assembly both reflects and is likely to reinforce the movement towards a Welsh dimension in policy formulation.

The replacement of Compulsory Competitive Tendering (CCT) by Best Value in Wales should be seen in this context. The new policy has been shaped by initiatives in England, but has also been influenced by the Welsh local government policy community. Furthermore, although the primary legislation on Best Value covers England and Wales, this is broad in scope and leaves substantial discretion to the Welsh Assembly to develop secondary legislation. Thus the nature of Best Value in the future is also likely to have a significant Welsh imprint.

In this paper we analyse the progress of Best Value in Wales, and examine the prospects for the implementation of the new framework for local service provision. In the first part we trace the origins and development of the distinctive aspects of the Welsh approach to Best Value. Then the paper outlines the services that are being piloted by 21 unitary authorities, one police authority and one fire authority, and identified the methods used by Welsh authorities in their 1998 service reviews. Our conclusions are based on an evaluation of councils' pilot bids and performance plans, and extensive discussions and interviews with numerous participants in the Best Value process in Wales, both in central and local government. The interview programme has covered all of the Welsh pilot authorities, and has included elected members, chief executives, senior managers in pilot services and front-line staff. Our formal role as the research team commissioned to undertake the Wales Evaluation Study on Best Value has also provided us with excellent access to documents and meetings.

At the outset it is important to note that the role of the Welsh pilots may have a broader significance for Best Value in England. The presence of Welsh authorities in the pilot programme is disproportionate to their number in local government as a whole. First, although Welsh authorities comprise only six per cent of all councils in England and Wales, they comprise almost 38 per cent of all pilot authorities. Secondly, the Welsh share of total pilot services is 37 per cent (approximately 127 pilot services in Wales, and 220 in England). Furthermore, the implementation of Best Value is proceeding more swiftly in Wales than in England. For example, Welsh pilots produced their first performance plans in April 1998, a year ahead of their English counterparts. Thus the Welsh Best Value pilots may be in a strong position to contribute not only to developments in Wales, but also to the national policy framework. If so, this will reverse the traditional flow of influence from English to Welsh local government.

THE DEVELOPMENT OF BEST VALUE IN WALES

The intention to replace CCT with a requirement to obtain Best Value was part of the manifesto commitment of the Labour Party: 'councils should not be forced to put their services out to tender, but will be required to obtain best value. Every council will be required to publish a local performance plan with targets for service improvement, and be expected to achieve them' (Labour Party, 1997). At this stage there were already differences in the CCT regime between England and Wales as a result of local government reorganisation. In Wales, there had been a CCT moratorium since April 1994, which was due to end in October 1997. In England, however, there was a moratorium only for those councils that were reorganised, with the remainder subject to the provisions of the 1980 and 1988 Acts. In June 1997 the moratorium on CCT in Wales was further extended by one year to October 1998. The Secretary of State for Wales indicated that he would like to develop the framework for piloting Best Value in advance of its introduction on a statutory basis (Welsh Office, 1998b). Best Value was also introduced in England at this time but there was no general moratorium on CCT.

At this stage the 12 'Principles of Best Value' were published by the government (DETR, 1997). These principles were further developed in Wales during July and August 1997 into a more detailed framework which could be used to pilot Best Value. This framework was devised by a Project Group which was set up jointly by the Welsh Office and the Welsh Local Government Association (WLGA) at the meeting of the Welsh Consultative Council of Local Government Finance (WCCLGF) on 16 July 1997. The project group is made up of individuals from the Welsh Office, the WLGA, the Audit Commission, District Audit, Wales TUC, and CBI Wales and is co-chaired by the WLGA and officials from the Welsh Office.[1] The remit of the group is to advise on, and manage, the development, testing and implementation of Best Value in Wales.

Selection of the Pilots

In August 1997 the Project Group published its report on 'A Framework for Developing Best Value in Welsh Local Government' (Project Group, 1997). This included a definition of Best Value as follows: 'Best Value and quality provision are achieved in an authority when services are responsive to changing needs and expectations of local people; consistently meet measurable, regularly improved and affordable performance targets; and are provided at demonstrably competitive prices' (Project Group, 1997). The report also provided the working framework of Best Value and proposals for testing the framework. The Secretary of State accepted the group's recommendations in September and invited local authorities in Wales (including police authorities and combined fire authorities) to submit proposals for involvement in the Wales Evaluation Study. At the outset there was a preference for many authorities to be involved: 'all authorities should be encouraged to submit proposals for involvement in a Wales-wide evaluation study' (Project Group, 1997). This was evident in the approach used by the Project Group. For example, a number of seminars were used to provide information and guidance on Best Value to authorities interested in submitting a proposal to pilot. In addition, there was a two-stage process of selection for pilot status in Wales. Authorities were invited to submit proposals by 31 October 1997, and 26 had done so by this date. These were appraised by the Project Group, against criteria specified in the framework document: commitment from the whole council; the quality of the proposal; and the extent to which the recent experience of the authority would enable early and effective implementation of their proposals. Members of the group were divided into teams to evaluate proposals and to work with particular authorities. This was done during November, and proposals were refined by authorities after guidance from their 'mentor' in the group.

The Project Group recommended that 23 proposals should be included in the Wales Evaluation Study. This was accepted by the Secretary of State and details of the authorities involved were reported on 4 December 1997. The selection process was different to that in England, partly because English councils which won pilot status would be exempt from the 1988 CCT legislation. There, an evaluation panel was set up to select the pilots. Only 37 bids were chosen, which represents around a quarter of English pilot bids (Martin, 1999). As a result of the sheer number of English authorities, the approach was not inclusive, but competitive.

Distinctive Aspects of Best Value in Wales

One of the key differences between England and Wales in the testing of Best Value is the partnership approach between central and local government in Wales. Previous research has highlighted the close and consultative relationships that exist between the Welsh Office and local authority staff (Boyne et al., 1991). In part, this reflects the small number of local authorities in Wales. As Osmond (1985: 28) states, 'it is possible for Welsh Office civil servants to establish personal relationships and acquire detailed knowledge of just 45 councils in a way that it is much more difficult for the Department of the Environment officials who have to deal with hundreds of local authorities in England'. The reorganisation of these 45 authorities into 22 has served to make this even easier. This close co-operation is evident in the decision that the Welsh Office and the WLGA would co-chair the Project Group, develop the framework to test Best Value together, and jointly fund the evaluation study. By contrast, in England the Local Government Association has had little direct involvement with the pilot schemes. The close central–local relationship is illustrated in the comment made by the Secretary of State for Wales that

> This ambitious objective can only be achieved through a partnership approach with local government. It is in this spirit that the initiative is being taken forward in Wales. The Welsh Local Government Association has given its enthusiastic welcome to the proposals and has played a major part in developing them in partnership with the Welsh Office and representatives of the Wales TUC, CBI Wales and the Audit Commission. (Welsh Office, 1997b)

Similarly, in its response to the Best Value consultation paper, the WLGA (1998: para.1.1.1), notes that it has been 'a positive partner with the Welsh Office … in developing a framework for improving local services through best value'.

In addition, the pilot authorities have a close working relationship with the Project Group, both collectively and individually. A number of mechanisms have been set up to support authorities involved in the Wales Evaluation Study and to help their collective evaluation of the framework that they are implementing. These include the Project Group, which continues to meet on a monthly basis. In addition, each pilot authority has nominated a project manager and these individuals meet collectively each month with members of the Project Group. Individual members of the Project Group also continue to be responsible for maintaining communication with a sub-group of project managers. Furthermore, a member of the Wales Evaluation Study research team attends the meetings of the Project Group and their meeting with the project managers. This contrasts with the situation in England where pilot authorities are involved in meetings with the evaluation team, but do not have regular contact with the evaluation panel.

Although there are close relationships between central and local government in Wales, there are areas where difficulties have arisen. One of these has been CCT. In Wales there was a view from the Project Group that the process of Best Value 'should not be compromised by a direct linkage with decisions on the future role and management of CCT in Wales' (Project Group, 1997). Hence councils selected as pilots did not gain the automatic exemption from CCT that those in England did. The existing moratorium on CCT was extended as a result of the progress that the pilots had made in developing Best Value: 'We have reviewed the progress they have made with Best Value and have been impressed by the substantial progress made in a short period and by the commitment demonstrated'

(Welsh Office, 1998b). However, additional information was requested by the Welsh Office before the orders for the moratorium could be established. This included a confirmation from the authorities that they were committed to the principles of competition, a statement of the test of competitiveness for the pilot services, information on processes of competition in services outside the scope of the Wales Evaluation Study, and an update on the expected outcome for those authorities which failed to reach the prescribed financial objective for work carried out in 1996–97. This continuing emphasis on competitive tendering was opposed by some local politicians, and threatened to cause difficulties for the pilot programme in Wales. These problems are now resolved, and authorities are proceeding with the implementation of Best Value.

PILOT SERVICES IN THE WALES EVALUATION STUDY

A total of 127 services have been selected by the pilot authorities to test the Best Value framework in the Wales Evaluation Study (Figure 1). The pilots include front-line and support services, CCT and non-CCT areas, and white-collar and blue-collar services. Several of the services are being piloted by more than one authority. For example, housing management, personnel and training, and education have been selected by six authorities; residential care homes for older people, sports and leisure services, and chief executive services have been selected by five authorities; and highways maintenance and grounds maintenance are being piloted in four authorities. Central services are the largest proportion of Welsh pilot services (22.8 per cent), whereas environmental management and technical services are the smallest (both comprise 7.1 per cent of all Welsh pilot services).

To what extent are the pilot services representative of the activities of Welsh local government? There are some differences between the composition of pilot services and the pattern of spending in Welsh local government, as indicated by gross capital and gross current expenditure data (Welsh Office, 1995; 1996). For instance, education constitutes 11.8 per cent of total Welsh pilot services, whereas it is approximately one-third of Welsh local government expenditure. This discrepancy may be attributed to the exclusion of schools from the Wales Evaluation Study – the pilots focus on central LEA functions. Similarly, police and fire authorities account for 11.0 per cent of total Welsh local government expenditure, but comprise 4.7 per cent of Welsh pilot services. This simply reflects the participation of a single police and a single fire authority in the Wales Evaluation Study. These discrepancies can be contrasted with the similarities between expenditure and presence in the pilot programme for two of the pilot services, namely social services (12.6 per cent of services and 11.3 per cent of expenditure) and technical services (7.1 per cent of services and 6.8 per cent of expenditure).

The wide range of functions selected to test the Best Value framework reflects the variety of approaches used by councils in choosing the individual services. Some adopted an 'authority-wide' approach, others identified broad service areas or more specific components of services, and still others selected services on the basis of matching service provision with community need. In contrast to the position in England, there are few 'cross-cutting' pilots in Wales. Most of the pilots remain in their 'service silos', but this is likely to change as service reviews develop. Is there any indication that authorities selected the pilot services on an *ad hoc* or planned basis? In order to answer this question we next outline the arguments presented in councils' pilot bids.

In developing the Best Value framework the underlying rationale of central government was that 'poorer performing services' would be reviewed first. Thus, where there was *prima facie* evidence that the authority's services were performing poorly, either against its own standards or in comparison with other authorities, then these services would be targeted first. The Welsh Office adopted a slightly different approach to the assessment of pilot bids: 'proposals should be evaluated and selected mainly on the basis of the quality of the submissions and their collective capacity to test the Best Value framework *across a good range* of local government activity' (Welsh Office, 1997a: 17, emphasis added).

A review of the pilot bids and performance plans provides some evidence that poor or weak performers were selected by five authorities. These services were regarded as either: (a) offering the potential for improvement and yielding better results (for example, a revenue services pilot); (b) not achieving the Welsh average costs per unit of output (for example, a catering services pilot); or (c) 'being sub-standard and unacceptable as a public service' (a land charges pilot). There was, however, a variety of arguments supporting service selection, and these are summarised below.

The 'Whole Authority' Approach

Three Welsh authorities have adopted a 'whole authority' approach (Cardiff, Swansea, Torfaen), arguing that this is necessary if the Best Value framework is to be successfully introduced and tested. One authority, for example, stated in its pilot bid that Best Value requires a fundamental shift away from the traditional 'producer-based' culture to a more 'consumer-based' culture. They reasoned that successfully implementing such cultural changes requires an 'authority wide' approach in order for new values and

FIGURE 1
WALES EVALUATION STUDY PILOT SERVICES

	Housing & Property Services	Central Services & Control	Planning, Development	Leisure & Culture	Social services	Environmental management	Technical services	Education, libraries	Police/Fire Authorities
	• Housing management • Housing maintenance repairs (5) • Rent collection • Property services (3) • Housing agency services	• Legal services • Internal audit • Corporate finance • Centre services • Housing benefits (2) • IT services (2) • Procurement • Finance (2) • Personnel /training services (6) • Chief Executive (5) • Exchequer services (3) • Unified benefits & advisory services • Revenue services	• Development control (3) • Assistance to small firms • Public protection (2) • Food safety • Environment Health (2) • Health & Safety • Planning (2) • Building control • Trading standards • Security • Occupational health (2) • Assistance to small firms • Community strategies • Consumer protection	• Community centers/halls • Sports & Leisure services (5) • Tourism	• Residential care homes (5) • Day care centres • Home care (2) • Catering (3) • Services visually impair • Social services (3) • Social services transportation	• Grounds maintenance (4) • Waste management (2) • Cleansing services • Refuse collection (2)	• Highways maintenance (4) • Engineering services • Road safety education • Traffic management • Transport management/ maintenance (2)	• Educational statementing • Library services (2) • School support services • Early years' education • Student awards • Special educational needs • General Education (6) • Home-school transport • Library services to housebound	• Hydrant maintenance • Legal services • Transport maintenance • Occupation l health • Staff training • Health & Safety
Number of Services	16	29	20	7	16	9	9	15	6
% of Total Pilot Services	12.6%	22.8%	15.8%	5.5%	12.6%	7.1%	7.1%	11.8%	4.7%

beliefs to become embedded and adopted by the workforce. Another authority argued that the whole authority approach provided an opportunity to:

> test [and/or] develop the [Best Value] framework in ways which are difficult if not impossible to accomplish through a focus on individual aspects or services. [Furthermore] within a "whole authority" approach, it is possible ... to identify some particular areas or services which might eliminate or help develop certain aspects of the [Best Value] framework.

However, two authorities argued that a 'whole authority' approach is not necessary for testing the Best Value framework. For example, they stated that they intend to use a whole authority approach in adopting the *principles* of Best Value, but do not intend to use this in *testing* the Best Value framework. It is important to note that there is a high degree of ambiguity when classifying authorities as 'whole authority' pilots. This designation does not imply that authorities are piloting every element of service provision. If the *number* of services piloted by 'non-whole authority' and 'whole authority' bids are compared, it becomes apparent that the distinction between the two groups is blurred. Several 'non-whole' authorities are piloting a similar number or, in some cases, more services, than the whole authority pilots. For example, one of the whole authority pilots covers only four or five services, whereas six authorities are piloting more than five services.

Adding further confusion to the whole authority issue is that some of the councils in this category intend to undertake some service reviews during 1999 rather than 1998, thereby placing the services outside the remit of the Wales Evaluation Study. This is clearly indicated by one of the whole authority pilots:

> All services of the County Council will be required to comply with this programme and respond to the requirements of the model and to demonstrate this in a structured and consistent manner. *This does not imply however, that the County Council or its Service Committees can, or will be able to, address every aspect contained within the model immediately or even within the time scale of this programme. Priorities and resources will determine what can be achieved. It does, however, imply that each aspect will be positively considered and appropriate decisions taken.* (Pilot Bid, emphasis original)

Selection of Individual Services

The following arguments were provided by authorities who have opted to target specific services to test the Best Value framework:

Testing the identified service will assist in implementing Best Value across the whole authority. Several authorities stated that the selected services offered the 'potential to assist the whole authority embrace the principles of Best Value'. Similarly one authority stated that the piloted services 'will provide a comprehensive test of Best Value' as part of the pilot study, which will form the basis for extending the Best Value model throughout the whole council.

It is noted by some authorities that introducing the principles of Best Value in certain service areas will present significant challenges. Therefore, piloting these 'challenging' services (for example, planning services in one authority) during the evaluation study will offer some insight when introducing the Best Value framework on an authority-wide basis.

The characteristics of the pilot services provide opportunities to test specific Best Value mechanisms. In some instances, authorities selected services that were considered to provide suitable settings in which to test the elements of Best Value. For example, one authority selected waste management services as it 'provides an excellent opportunity *to develop* and test a framework for wide consultation with the community', whereas another authority stated that it intends to build on the existing consultation processes used by its catering services. Similarly, two authorities based their selection of specific services (legal services and residential homes for the elderly) on the ease of implementing benchmarking.

Models of 'good practice'. It is the intention of some authorities to include a mix of services in the pilot study – those regarded as already having achieved 'good practice', and those identified as offering the potential for improvement. For example, one authority is piloting a mix of CCT and non-CCT services with the intention of building on the ostensible strengths of the processes involved in the former (for example, service specification and cost centre analysis), while avoiding its perceived weaknesses (for example, over-emphasis on price and clear differentiation between client and contractor). Furthermore, this authority hopes that the piloting process will provide a way of facilitating the 'cross-fertilisation' of ideas and experiences between services.

Community issues. Two authorities intend to use the Best Value framework to address specific community issues. For example, one authority is piloting leisure centres in an attempt to arrest the out-migration of young people from remote rural communities. Similarly, another authority has selected a variety of services to test the Best Value framework with the intention of achieving a closer alignment between service provision and local community need. The local communities within this council have diverse socio-economic profiles, and the authority argues that service provision should be more sensitive to the needs of each community rather than simply being provided on a council-wide basis.

Volunteers willing to participate in the study. There is little evidence in either the pilot bids or performance plans that authorities selected services on the basis of 'willing volunteers'. However, one authority stated that a 'small number of volunteers' was selected to take part in the pilot studies. Even though this authority relied on volunteers, it argued that the process of service selection was not undertaken in an arbitrary manner, but was based on a 'rigorous' framework for service selection. This included an employee forum in which all the potential pilot studies were considered, with the final decisions being based on 'meeting the requirements of testing the Best Value model'.

A cross-section of diverse services. Several authorities selected the pilot services on the basis that they offer diversity in testing the Best Value framework. For example, Wrexham is piloting: library services, building control, housing management and repair, security, community strategies, elderly person's homes and work opportunities for people with learning difficulties. The council anticipates that this approach will provide a means of exploring and overcoming obstacles faced by some services when introducing Best Value, with the potential benefits of applying the Best Value framework being shared across service areas.

THE IMPLEMENTATION OF BEST VALUE: PROSPECTS FOR SERVICE REVIEW

The prospects for the implementation of Best Value can be analysed at two levels: the inter- and intra-organisational. Inter-organisational issues are reflected in the standard 'top-down' model, which distinguishes between the making of policy and its implementation. In this case, the BV legislation has been developed by central government, and is to be implemented by local government. There is a substantial public policy literature which identifies the circumstances which are required for 'perfect implementation'. Hogwood and Gunn (1984) identify a number of essential factors, such as the availability of adequate time and resources, complete understanding and agreement on objectives, perfect communication between those involved, the ability of those in control to obtain perfect obedience, and preferably a single agency responsible for implementation. It is unlikely that these factors will all be present when BV becomes mandatory for all authorities in 2000. For example, there are a range of organisations who will be responsible for the implementation of BV: primarily local authorities, but also the Audit Commission, and in Wales and Scotland the assembly and the parliament.

Even if all the conditions for perfect inter-organisational implementation are met, there are additional circumstances at the intra-organisational level which may influence the introduction of BV. The literature on the 'management of change' suggests that a number of factors may be significant in the implementation of BV. These occur at the individual as well as the organisational level. Individuals may resist any change which threatens to have adverse economic implications, or simply be inconvenient for them. Reasons for organisational resistance can include, for example, a threat to the power or influence that certain groups have over information or decisions. BV clearly has the potential to shift power between individuals and groups within local government. Some councillors, for example, may perceive the increased emphasis on consumer evaluation as threatening their role as the primary conduit of public views.

The prospects for the implementation of BV are likely to vary across local authorities. This may reflect the extent to which they are receptive to change (Pettigrew et al. 1992). It may also reflect the extent to which the policy is a radical shift from past practice. It is likely that organisations and individuals who already have experience of some of the elements of BV will find them easier to implement. In an extreme case, an authority may already have been undertaking all of the BV processes and will simply have to parcel them together. Indeed, many managers in pilot services claim that BV processes were already in place, or are simply what they had planned to do anyway. The reality, however, is that important aspects of performance planning and service review are new to local councils.

Service reviews are seen as pivotal to the success of Best Value and the achievement of continuous improvement. As the WLGA (1997: 34) argues, 'the process of periodic in-depth service review will be the most potent tool for achieving improved service performance'. The reviews of pilot services in Wales started in April 1998. The expected outcome of each service review is an action plan which feeds directly into authorities' second performance plan. The results of the service review will be available to the public. The intention is that when Best Value is fully in place each service will be reviewed every four to five years. Decisions about the services to be reviewed each year will be left to the discretion of the local authority, though it is suggested that the sequence of reviews is based on expenditure (to ensure that 20 per cent of an authority's expenditure is covered annually) and/or areas of weakest performance (Welsh Office, 1998a).

The assessment of current service standards and the establishment of future targets are to be achieved through the Best Value mechanisms of user evaluation, employee evaluation, process benchmarking, tests of competitiveness and the use of indicators that allow authorities to track performance over time and between providers. For their 1998 performance plans, Welsh pilot authorities were asked to specify: service objectives and appropriate performance measures, an agenda for service review, the methodology of their reviews, and how the reviews will assist in promotion of equal opportunities and the Welsh language. Some authorities were unclear about Best Value processes, as indicated by the following statement from a Performance Plan: 'the relationship between the Performance Plan and the service reviews has proved perplexing for some of the pilots'. Nevertheless, each pilot authority set out proposals for service review in its performance plan. The government expects the reviews to be 'fundamental': 'each ... [service review] *challenges* the purpose of a service or group of services, *compares* the authority's performance both with that of others and with its own track record in previous years, *consults* the community and provides for *competition*, where appropriate' (Welsh Office, 1998a: emphasis original). It is to an appraisal of the prospects for service review that we now turn.

Performance Indicators

Two types of performance indicator are being used by Welsh pilots: national, to make comparisons between authorities; and local, to inform service providers and users about detailed performance. The performance indicators used in, and developed through, service review are expected to capture the entire process of service production – inputs, outputs and outcomes. There was an implicit assumption in the Best Value regime that authorities already use performance measures to manage their services, and that these can be drawn upon quickly to highlight areas of concern. However, our interviews with managers of pilot services suggest that this assumption is optimistic.

Authorities have identified a range of national data sources that they currently use, most frequently the Citizen's Charter. However, these do not cover the full range of council services. Furthermore, many of these are not valid measures of performance (Boyne, 1997a). Other national indicators include the DAWNING[2] data base and information annually requested from government departments, agencies or professional institutes.

The majority of authorities are working with a range of local performance data on inputs, efficiency and outputs. The development of new indicators is seen as an inclusive process: 'it is the council's intention to develop its own measures of performance and to involve the public and staff in this' (Welsh Best Value Pilot Authority); we will 'consult with all relevant parties and peer groups to establish relevant and meaningful performance indicators' (Welsh Best Value Pilot Authority). The lack of available performance indicators, particularly on quality and outcomes, will clearly impact on the ability of the pilots to fully implement this aspect of service review. Furthermore, such indicators will take time to develop as many pilot services will have to collect and analyse additional data.

User Evaluation

Authorities had developed a variety of consultation strategies prior to the introduction of BV, whether at the behest of government or as a result of local initiatives to understand users' views and bring decision-making closer to them (Burns *et al.*, 1994). Best Value places a responsibility upon local government to achieve 'genuine local accountability' (Welsh Office, 1998a), particularly through user involvement in the specification of performance indicators and targets. The emphasis on user evaluation is drawn directly from the 'in search of excellence' model of management (Peters and Waterman, 1982; Ferlie *et al.*, 1996; Walker, 1998).

The quality of user evaluation strategies outlined in the 1998 performance plans varied substantially, both between authorities and pilot services. For example, 13 authorities provided corporate statements on user evaluation (though not all were well articulated). Only two pilot authorities did not discuss user evaluation strategies in their performance plans. Over half of the pilots are undertaking resident surveys as part of their service review. Beyond the use of these survey instruments, the majority of authorities are adopting a range of communication channels with users. These include: feedback mechanisms (for example, focus groups, participation panels, surgeries); communications to residents (for example, newsletters); and procedures for responding to problems (for example, helplines, complaints procedures). Linkages are also being made with processes of quality assurance to ensure that residents views are taken on board. It is likely then that this aspect of service review will be relatively straightforward for most pilots to implement.

Employee Evaluation

The Best Value documentation (Welsh Office/WLGA, 1997; Welsh Office, 1998a), outlines models of human resource management which combine both 'hard' and 'soft' approaches (Storey, 1989). Hard approaches are expressed in the explicit and rationalistic link of human resources with financial resources to achieve business objectives. Soft approaches are seen in the emphasis on employees as valued assets and a source of competitive advantage, the role of employee commitment, and the importance of the quality of employees. For example: 'Staff possess a great deal of detailed and valuable knowledge about their area of service delivery. They have much to contribute in terms of how services can be improved' (Welsh Best Value Pilot Authority).

Many authorities emphasise communication, training and feedback to staff in order to ensure that the service reviews will be meaningful. Some authorities are developing specific service review strategies to involve their staff and to take their views into account. These, as with user evaluations, often build upon existing practice and therefore may develop rapidly as part of the service review. They include communication (seminars, the intranet), feedback mechanisms (staff surveys, meetings, focus groups), problem solving (quality circles) and appraisal (performance assessment interviews).

The acquisition of externally validated awards is seen an important demonstration of the commitment to employee evaluation. This is similarly reflected in the consultation paper (Welsh Office, 1998a). Most frequently cited are Investors in People (gained or in the process of accreditation by 13 Welsh pilot authorities) and the European Foundation for Quality Management Business Excellence Model (which is being explored by nine authorities).

Benchmarking

Whilst proposals for user and employee evaluations build on existing practice for authorities, benchmarking represents a newer management tool. Though the emphasis by the Best Value Project Group was on process benchmarking (Welsh Office/WLGA, 1997), benchmarking can also be concerned with costs and performance. The latter focus is highlighted in the consultation paper (Welsh Office, 1998a). Benchmarking is again a management process with private sector origins (Wolfram Cox *et al.*, 1997). The procedure is predicated upon continuous improvement through comparisons with high performing organisations, learning from them and setting improved standards based on the acquisition of this knowledge (Shetty, 1993).

Welsh authorities are developing a range of inter-authority and inter-organisational frameworks to benchmark their services. These include self-initiated benchmarking clubs where authorities compare services with each other and with private or voluntary providers. Consultants, professional institutes and the district audit service are facilitating these clubs in Wales. The district audit service has developed the DAWNING database which is intended to contain performance and cost data on all unitary authority services.

Councils in Wales are adopting a variety of approaches to benchmarking, but the overarching emphasis is upon understanding how their costs compare with other organisations. However, pilot authorities have concerns about sharing information with private sector organisations who may be competing to provide services if the outcome of a service review indicates the need for market testing. Consequently, the majority of comparisons are between authorities rather than with other providers. Authorities are also spending considerable time identifying common standards and definitions of services in order to ensure that any comparisons are meaningful. This aspect of service review is likely to be difficult for pilot authorities to implement as it is, for almost all, a new management tool.

Tests of Competitiveness

This is proving to be one of the most difficult aspects of review. Best Value maintains the emphasis of the policies of the previous government on a diversity of providers, and on the strengths of partnerships with the private and voluntary sectors. There is a presumption that services should be 'exposed periodically to competition, except where authorities have been able to demonstrate that this would be inappropriate'. Nevertheless, '[t]he Government has no intention of returning to the mechanistic and inflexible approach to contracting characterised by CCT' (Welsh Office, 1998a: 19).

Authorities are exploring a number of approaches to demonstrate the competitiveness of their services. One authority claims to have demonstrated the competitiveness of its services through a contract it had won in the open market, and others are exploring partnership arrangements in their service reviews. The use of benchmarking as a test of competitiveness poses difficulties. An authority's service may be provided economically and efficiently when compared to other authorities, but this does not rule out the possibility that the performance of other organisations may be even better. It may therefore prove difficult for pilot authorities to argue for any test of competitiveness other than open market testing.

Welsh pilot services have a range of prior experiences with competition. For example, blue-collar services are accustomed to market testing, through compulsion rather than choice, whereas white-collar services in Wales are not. Other services have been exposed to 'contestability' rather than compulsory competition. For example, LEAs do not have a captive market in the provision of specialist services to schools; individual schools have the option of seeking alternative suppliers. Other services, such as social services, have been obliged to create and stimulate an external market. The experience of competition varies not only across local services, but also between geographical areas. The range of alternative suppliers of local services is generally higher in large urban areas than in small rural authorities. For some services, more recently exposed to competition, there is little or no market. For example, one authority argued in its performance plan that there is 'no identifiable Housing Management market' (Welsh Best Value Pilot Authority).

Tests of competitiveness have been strongly debated since the establishment of the Welsh framework for Best Value. The extension of the CCT moratorium was dependent upon authorities providing written confirmation that they were committed to competition. The emphasis upon market testing in a policy originally identified as replacing CCT has left authorities grappling with the role of competition within their service reviews.

CONCLUSION

The Best Value pilot programme in Wales has developed rapidly in its first year. The pace of the reform has been driven by the concern of the Welsh Office and the Welsh Local Government Association to tailor Best Value to the circumstances of local authorities in Wales. The desire to be seen to take a lead in policy formulation may also anticipate the need for both bodies to demonstrate this capacity to the Welsh Assembly. A consequence of this 'pioneering spirit' is that Welsh councils are constantly confronting the boundaries of the known Best Value universe. They have had to answer questions to which central government, professional bodies and academic researchers have no clear answers. For example: what is a performance plan? How should users be consulted for the purposes of service review? Which measures of performance are appropriate to the Best Value framework? What is the difference between a test of competitiveness and competitive tendering?

Initially, some of the pilot authorities were perplexed by the apparent failure of central government to furnish definitive responses to these problems. Indeed, there was a suspicion that these were 'trick questions', and that the answers were already known by the Welsh Office. Gradually, however, some officers and members have come to realise that Best Value is different from CCT in one important respect: the broad agenda may have been set by central government, but, as yet, there is no detailed set of regulations for local authorities to follow. In Wales in particular, there appears to be some scope for a genuine partnership between central and local government in developing and testing the Best Value framework. Whether this results in the continuous improvements to local services that the Labour government is seeking remains to be seen.

NOTES

1. A member of the Wales Evaluation Research Team joined the Project Group after the award of the research contract in February 1998. A representative of the Local Government Management Board also joined the Group in 1998.
2. The DAWNING database provides comparative data by which Welsh authorities can compare their performance with other Welsh authorities

REFERENCES

Boyne, G.A., 1997a, 'Comparing the Performance of Local Authorities: An Analysis of the Audit Commission Indicators', *Local Government Studies* Vol.23, No.4, pp.17–43.

Boyne, G.A., 1997b, 'Public Choice Theory and Local Government Structure: An Evaluation of Local Government Reorganisation in Scotland and Wales', *Local Government Studies* Vol.23, No.3, pp.56–72.

Boyne, G.A. *et al.*, 1991, *Local Government in Wales. Its Role and Function* (York: Joseph Rowntree Foundation).

Burns, D., R. Hambleton and P. Hoggett, 1994, *The Politics of Decentralisation: Revitalising Local Democracy* (London: Macmillan).

DETR, 1997, *The 12 Principles of Best Value* (London: DETR).

DETR, 1998, *Modernising Local Government: Improving Local Services through Best Value* (London: DETR).

Farrell, C. and J. Law, 1998, 'Regional Policy Differences in the UK: Education in Wales', *Public Policy and Administration*.

Ferlie, E. *et al.*, 1996, *The New Public Management in Action* (Oxford: Oxford University Press).

Hogwood, B.W. and L.A. Gunn, 1984, *Policy Analysis for Real World* (Oxford: Oxford University Press).

Labour Party, 1997, *New Labour because Wales Deserves Better* (Labour Party Manifesto).

Martin, S., 1998, 'A Preliminary Analysis of Bids for Inclusion in the Best Value Pilot Programme' (paper presented at Public Services Research Unit Conference, Cardiff University, March).

Osmond, J., 1985, 'The Dynamic of Institutions', in J. Osmond (ed.), *The National Question Again – Welsh Political identity in the 1980s* (Dyfed: Gomer).

Peters, T.J. and R.H. Waterman, Jr., 1982, *In Search of Excellence, Lessons from America's Best Run Companies* (New York: Harper and Row).

Pettigrew, A., E. Ferlie and L. McKee, 1992, *Shaping Strategic Change* (London: Sage).

Project Group, 1997, *A Framework for Developing Best Value in Welsh Local Government* (Cardiff: Welsh Office).

Shetty, Y.K., 1993, 'Aiming High: Competitive Benchmarking for Superior Performance', *Long Range Planning* 1, pp.39–44.

Storey, J. (ed.), 1989, *New Perspectives on Human Resource Management* (London: Routledge).

Walker, R.M., 1998, 'New Public Management and Housing Associations: From Comfort to Competition', *Policy and Politics* 26, pp.71–87.

Welsh Local Government Association, 1998, *Response to Welsh Office Consultation Paper: 'Modernising Local Government in Wales* (Cardiff: WLGA).

Welsh Office, 1995, *Welsh Local Government Financial Statistics* (Cardiff: Welsh Office).

Welsh Office, 1996, *Welsh Local Government Financial Statistics* (Cardiff: Welsh Office).

Welsh Office, 1997a, *A Framework for Developing Best Value in Welsh Local Government: The First Report of the Best Value Project Group* (Cardiff: Welsh Office).

Welsh Office, 1997b, 'Ron Davies Wants Local Government to Test Best Value Proposals' (Press Release, Welsh Office, September).

Welsh Office, 1998a, *Modernising Local Government in Wales: Improving Local Services through Best Value* (Cardiff: Welsh Office).

Welsh Office, 1998b, 'Win Griffiths Extends the Moratorium on Re-introducing Compulsory Competitive Tendering' (Press Release, 22nd May).

Welsh Office/WLGA, 1997, *A Framework for Developing Best Value in Welsh Local Government. The First Report of the Best Value Project Group, Revised* (Cardiff: Welsh Office/WLGA).

Wolfram Cox, J.R., L. Mann and D. Samson, 1997, 'Benchmarking as a Mixed Metaphor: Disentangling Assumptions of Competition and Collaboration', *Journal of Management Studies* 34, pp.285–314.

Developing Best Value in Scotland: Concepts and Contradictions

ARTHUR MIDWINTER and NEIL McGARVEY

Labour's commitment to the Best Value approach in policy terms has still permitted significant differences of practice in Scotland. The argument is made here that Best Value incorporates elements of the rationales behind both CCT and performance management. It is not therefore a radical break from past practice – more of an incremental change which builds on initiatives of recent years. The article concludes that there are unresolved tensions and contradictions which need to be addressed if the policy is to have a significant and lasting impact on the day-to-day practices of Scottish local councils.

Labour's Best Value in Scotland is more comprehensive than England with all councils being required to demonstrate that a Best Value management regime is in place through self-documentation, and all 32 Scottish councils are presently about to undertake their first yearly self-assessment. Unlike south of the border there has been no piloting. However, the prospect of external validation by the Scottish Office and the Accounts Commission in future years is a strong one.

In Scotland after the 1997 election the government extended the moratorium on Compulsory Competitive Tendering (CCT) provided existing tendering was completed. The reintroduction of CCT was suspended within one month of the Labour victory, whilst the essential elements of a Best Value regime were developed by a joint Scottish Office/Accounts Commission/Convention of Scottish Local Authorities (COSLA) Task Force.

The Scottish approach stemmed from a political desire to be tough as regards maintaining competition as a disciplining force in councils. The Scottish Office talked of 'appropriate enforcement procedures and sanctions will have to be in place over the longer term before CCT can be abolished through primary legislation' (Scottish Office circular 22, 1997). CCT has not been abandoned – those councils not measuring up to the requirements

Arthur Midwinter and Neil McGarvey, University of Strathclyde.

of Best Value management face the prospect of its reintroduction. Authorities were able to secure exemption from CCT if they had demonstrated significant progress towards Best Value. In developing Best Value there was a desire in the Scottish Office to promote a new partnership approach with local councils. The vision is of a co-operative and constructive relationship. COSLA agreed to this approach and to participate in a Task Force which would outline the key principles and essential elements. The end result is that every council in Scotland is required, through self-documentation and assessment, to demonstrate 'Best Value' – the prize for fulfilling such a procedure being exemption from CCT legislation.

THE ORIGINS OF BEST VALUE

In the British context, the roots of Best Value as a policy itself are a testament to the *ad hoc* nature of policy development and formation. The words began to appear intermittently in the speeches and sound bites of shadow Labour ministers when the subject of local government was discussed during the year prior to the 1997 general election . The Labour Manifesto commitment was that 'Councils will be required to obtain best value ... We reject the dogmatic view that services must be privatised to be of high quality, but equally we see no reason why a service should be delivered directly if other more efficient means can be found' (Labour Party, 1997).

In terms of policy formulation, Best Value as a concept was developed by the English Association of District Councils, Metropolitan Authorities and County Councils. A series of publications by Filkin clarified the concept (for example, Filkin, 1997a; 1997b). For Filkin, Best Value will develop in many ways as local authorities seek mechanisms and procedures to deliver quality public services in a more efficient and effective manner. Initially, the two most obvious ones – comparison and competition – would be used. The problem with the former is whether 'it is a powerful enough process to motivate change and improvement' (Filkin 1997a: 22). This is why competition has been given such emphasis, much to the surprise of many in local government (ibid.: 23).

In terms of formulation, the development of Best Value as a policy can be described as bottom-up – with the development of key concepts coming from within local government. However, councils which fail to measure up to the Best Value criteria as set out by the Scottish Office face the possible reintroduction of CCT.

Best Value is, of course, Labour's much-heralded replacement for CCT which compelled local authorities to invite tenders from private operators for a range of council services such as refuse collection, cleaning of buildings, street cleaning, schools and welfare catering, other catering, ground maintenance, vehicle repair and maintenance. In England, CCT had been more extensively developed by a bigger team in the Department of Environment. Its impact on Scotland, whilst still significant (especially in terms of internal restructuring), was not on the same scale as in England as regards the outsourcing of work (Midwinter, 1995).

It is always important to remember that few of the major core local government services were subject to CCT. Although the Act in 1988 which extended CCT provided statutory authority for a limitless extension of defined activities (thaaat is, those which should be subject to CCT), the only such extension in Scotland was to management of sport and leisure facilities in December 1989. In Scotland, like England and Wales, CCT was due to be extended to manual services such as cleaning police buildings, maintaining police and fire vehicles, home to school transport, direct public services such as management of theatres and art facilities, library support services, parking services, construction-related services – architecture, engineering, property management; as well as corporate services such as legal, personnel, financial and computing. This was suspended during the transition to the reformed unitary system. At the current time, around 25 per cent of local authority staff are employed under the CCT contract model.

In Scotland, the economic rationale behind CCT was never accepted by any beyond a small group of councils, and had few attractions for Scottish local government, which has become increasingly dominated by the Labour Party in the past 19 years. It was viewed as not delivering quality, value-for-money or continuous improvement. Most councils viewed CCT as a cumbersome process with too much regulation.

It was also argued that CCT undermined local democracy. It compelled councils to follow particular policies contrary to their wishes. There were concerns that policy initiatives in fields such as equal opportunities, industrial relations and anti-poverty were being compromised by the process. Moreover, it insulated council decision making associated with CCT from democratic processes. Small groups of councillors and officers are involved in the secretive bidding process with minimal public involvement. Also, by emphasising accountability through the market, CCT undermined the wider community basis of local government.

In terms of implementation, CCT caused many problems. Filkin (1997b) makes reference to problems such as adversarial procurement systems, price-based selection, short contracts, limited information about staff inherited under TUPE and contracts written to neutralise technological advantage. In Scotland, the reasons for opposition to CCT went beyond ideological opposition and regulatory practicalities. Like many other

Conservative-imposed policies in the 1980s and 1990s, the legitimacy of imposing it on a population and in councils where Conservatives were so poorly represented was questioned. Moreover, in the Scottish rural hinterland, arguments about competition do not stand up as the conditions for competitive markets do not exist. In general, contracts tended to be much smaller and thus market stimulation was minimal. This, as well as the more forceful nature of the 'in-house commitment' in Scotland's local councils, is reflected in their success in maintaining a directly employed workforce by taking appropriate streamlining measures and forcing through 'necessary' reductions in wages. In Scotland, over 90 per cent of the contracts awarded under the 1988 Act were won on an in-house basis (Midwinter, 1995). (The 'in house' commitment still remains within many Scottish councils and it will be interesting to see how it influences market testing procedures as Best Value develops.)

Despite hostility to the whole CCT process, something approaching a consensus that cost savings were made has emerged in recent years (the problem for many Scottish councils was that these savings were derived, in the main, from reductions in wages, terms and conditions and the casualisation of work for those at the bottom end of the labour market). Although not having the same impact in terms of contracts awarded to external operators, CCT did result in major internal restructuring within Scotland's councils. Client/contractor splits resulted in clear specification of services and in most cases a lowering, as well as improved awareness, of costs. Thus, despite the hostility by which CCT was greeted and implemented in Scotland, most are now agreed that CCT did deliver benefits in terms of the specification of services.

Other positive features retained under the Best Value regime include the monitoring of performance against specifications, as well as the firm control over payments and costs. Best Value seeks to eliminate the rigidity and inflexibility of CCT. Whereas CCT demanded compliance to the letter of the law as set out in acts of parliament, Best Value demands commitment to its principles, requiring councils to be what one Scottish local council director described as 'enthusiastic, flexible and creative' (SLGIU, 1997). Whereas councils were antagonistic and legalistic in their approach to CCT, the hope is that a spirit of partnership will eventually prevail.

An important point to note is that it was not only those in the public sector who were antagonistic towards CCT. As Rees notes,

> Much of the private sector with experience in contracting with local authorities now agree CCT has become a game not worth playing. In common with the rest of the industry, they would prefer to look for a longer term partnership between the authority as procurer and themselves as supplier. They realise an adversarial relationship is not

to the benefit of their employees and shareholders nor does it serve the interests of the authority and local taxpayers. (Rees, 1996: 64)

In a similar vein, at a recent Association of Direct Labour Organisations Seminar, Stelio Stefanou – the Chair of the CBI Local Government Procurement Panel – argued that compulsion had fostered uncertainty and damaged the quality of services. Frank McAveety, leader of Glasgow City Council expressed similar sentiments (ADLO, 1998).

The consensus in both public and private sector circles appears to be that relationships between client and contractor must more accurately reflect practice in the private sector where the emphasis is on trust in the long term partnerships. As Walsh has argued, if contracts are to be efficient as a means of managing public services then more extensive trust based relationships are likely to be necessary to underpin them (see Walsh, 1995: 49–52). Overall, comparing Best Value to CCT, its application will be more comprehensive than CCT – extending, as it does, to all council services. The intention is to establish processes, systems and a management culture which generate ongoing service improvements in service delivery. Central government today is much more ambivalent as regards the appropriate public/private sector mix in relation to service delivery, and competition, whilst still viewed as essential, is but one tool among many to improve quality and value. However, Best Value retains the same commitment as CCT to service specification, performance monitoring and strict financial controls.

Best Value also has its roots in many of the ideas associated with the performance management agenda which has impacted heavily on local government in recent years. The question of how local councils perform has very much come to the fore in local government over the past decade. The specification, measurement and evaluation of the performance of the council has come under increasing scrutiny. Initially, at least, the techniques of performance management were seen as alternatives to CCT to be used in non-contracting services. As Pollitt notes, 'performance assessment ... would be a suitable discipline for those parts of the public sector that could not be privatised or subjected directly to the sanitising forces of the market' (Pollitt, 1986: 159).

Initiatives associated with the new performance agenda included the development of statutory performance indicators and the extension of the Accounts Commission auditing remit. In essence, many of these techniques could be labelled 'competition by comparison' (Biggs and Dunleavy, 1995: 686) – local authorities were 'competing' to better their own past performance, external judgements on performance, as well as that of other comparable councils.

Many Scottish councils were initially hostile to some of these new techniques. Economy seemed to be the driving force for the Scottish Office. Whereas existing data systems included much detail as regards information which could be translated into indicators for economy and efficiency, there was a lack of effectiveness indicators. Pollitt suggests that the neglect of effectiveness indicators was part of a 'play-it-safe' strategy as auditors and managers sought to avoid the politically troublesome areas of outcome and quality (Pollitt, 1990).

In practice, performance indicators perform well below the managerial rhetoric of their advocates. Indicators are selected on a judgemental basis and offer little real insight into organisational efficiency. Their development remains problematic and 'the problem is with the model and its imposition on the bureaucracy by the political process' (Midwinter, 1995: 51). These limitations have been played down in their incorporation into Best Value. The processes of benchmarking, the development of service plans and targets for performance are all key features of Best Value and can be linked back to this performance agenda which existed in the 1980s and early 1990s. Many of the ideas and practices of it, it would seem, are to be enshrined in Best Value.

Performance management is also linked to accountability, and those focusing on performance tend to stress the benefits of increased financial and managerial accountability. Targets, charters and PIs were all viewed as new policy instruments to increase transparency, and thus accountability, in local service provision. Financial reforms, structural reorganisations and policy initiatives have invariably been heralded as improving the accountability of local authorities. From the reformist perspective there thus seems to be a recognition of accountability as a problem. The democratic renewal agenda employs many similar arguments.

The new management agenda sees the problem as rooted in the functional nature of local councils (SOLACE, 1994). The bureaucratic organisational form was concerned only with honesty, integrity, impartiality and objectivity and how rules and processes could be devised to ensure officers exhibited these characteristics. Traditionally, the emphasis in auditing was on legality and propriety: money was spent where it was allowed and was accounted for retrospectively.

The Prime Minister regards the traditional model as incompatible with his desire for a strong executive providing clear leadership. To quote: 'The new ways of working should also involve council officers as well as council members. Senior managers must provide clear vision and leadership to their staff. They need to challenge and breakdown those professional and departmental barriers that hold back innovation and modernisation' (Blair, 1997: 17). Just what this modernisation is in practice is still unclear. The old ways are bad, but how they adversely affected services requires further exposition and explanation. However, under the Best Value regime, accountability requires simple and robust information across the full range of local government services to demonstrate performance. It also requires that customers have an opportunity to influence decisions about services. Best Value councils as a matter of course should allow the public more opportunity to contribute to and influence decisions. In essence, Best Value is presented as another solution to the perennial problem of local accountability.

BEST VALUE IN SCOTLAND: THE KEY CONCEPTS

Best Value seems to be defined as many things. At different times it is defined as a process rather than a product; description rather than prescription; a search for continuous improvement; a means of promoting change in attitudes, culture and management style within councils. There remains a certain woolliness about it. Best Value is in essence an amalgam of accumulated wisdom and orthodoxy as regards management practice. It has taken the positive and negative lessons learned from CCT and performance-related exercises and moulded together a local government best practice model of management. In the remainder of this section, we summarise the official vision of Best Value as set out in various task group reports.

In the context of council services, the Task Force see value as a concept which is capable of analysis and expression (if not definition). A Best Value regime will require councils to produce meaningful and robust information to allow those who benefit from and pay for council services to judge performance. The Task Force emphasises this need for a more rigorous approach to assessing performance in local government:

> The disciplines of clearly specifying services, monitoring performance and keeping sound control of payments and costs were positive outcomes of CCT and should be retained under Best Value. Indeed Best Value should seek to spread these practices throughout all council work. However, the rigidity of tendering and the lack of flexibility were not attractive features of CCT. The divisiveness and duplication which often accompanied CCT are also features which Best Value hopes to eliminate, by developing a more corporate, more comprehensive and fairer approach to council services. Best Value does not signal a return to the past. Rather it seeks to build on past experience in a positive and rigorous fashion to ensure that citizens receive the very best from the resources available to councils. (Scottish Office/COSLA, 1997: para.1.5)

As noted, Best Value in Scotland has been worked up by a small Task Force consisting of Scottish Office civil servants, COSLA officials and a representative from the Accounts Commission. From initial Scottish Office documentation, the perception was that Best Value would enshrine:

good managment practices – strategic and seervice planning, budgetary and financial control;

planning for improvement – Best Value is linked to continuous improvement with emphasis on quality improvement, cost reduction and greater efficiency;

tools for improvement – how management tools, especially a significant degree of competition sensibly applied might deliver Best Value.

The Task Force's initial definition of the essential elements of Best Value viewed it as incorporating the key elements of sound governance, performance measurement and monitoring, continuous improvement, and long term planning and budgeting.

Sound governance needs, firstly, a customer/citizen focus to assess customer satisfaction, priorities and preferences. This requires the involvement of the public in the specification of service standards as well as evaluation of performance, through mechanisms such as public meetings, decentralised area forums, newsletters, questionnaires, complaints procedures, citizens juries. The involvement of the public should increase understanding of the constraints councils are working under. It also requires sound strategic management, with councils setting, communicating and monitoring their broad values, aims and objectives. This requires a clear and coherent articulation of corporate strategy. Statements of core values do not constitute strategies – they need to be interpreted for individual services.

Sound operational management to ensure that these strategic aims are achieved through service planning with performance and financial monitoring is also central. Service departmental strategy and service planning should be informed by the values which the council aspires to. In other words, service plans are the mechanisms through which the council's values are translated into concrete, operational objectives the achievement of which can serve as indicators of performance.

Sound financial management with rigorous costing systems should be extended to all areas of local government. This requires monitoring and information systems which ensure that the right information is made available to managers in the right format and at the right time. The council has a sound budgetary control information system with monitoring and year-end projections by accountable managers. Are there budgetary and financial controls in place to ensure that financial disciplines are observed while achieving those aims? It should also ensure service plans are realistic in light of resources. Overall sound financial management requires a linkage between what the council is seeking to achieve and plans and budgets. The Angus Council Best Value document links up the key features of sound governance: 'In general Service Plans are prepared having regard to customer consultation and following staff participation ... The Plans relate key themes to targets ... Challenging but achievable levels take into account likely budgetary position of the department' (Angus Council, 1997: 13)

Performance management and monitoring is also a key feature of Best Value. Best Value requires that performance information for internal management purposes is available in valid, reliable and timely formats. It requires that the council develops and makes use of its own performance information within and across councils. The right information must be available to the right person at the right time in the right format to allow informed decision making. The council should be able to demonstrate progress against targets.

Through service plans the council should ensure performance information is specific, measurable, action-oriented, realistic and time-scaled. In the longer term these performance plans will cover all services and be linked to three-year budgets. They will set targets for service and budget levels. The argument of the Scottish Task Force is that 'As Best Value develops, the concept will gain an ever sharper profile, supported by systems and audit techniques which assess cost, quality, standards and performance measures' (Scottish Office/COSLA, 1997: para.2.1).

If the mechanisms of sound governance and performance monitoring are in place, councils will have the basis of ensuring continuous improvement in council services. However, other mechanisms of utility in this respect include clear costing procedures with clear financial management information systems at various levels of detail, and a businesslike CCT approach to costing input and outputs for all services; benchmarking as a tool for comparing the cost-effectiveness, performance and processes of a service against the private sector, other services, other councils and external databases; and rigorous option appraisal exercises for large capital schemes and projects with major revenue implications in all services. The Task Force suggests that councils should continually ask themselves five essential questions: What are we seeking to do? Why are we doing it? How are we doing it? Are we achieving our goals? Can we get better?

Overall, if the mechanisms of sound governance are in place and operating properly, councils would move towards long-term planning and budgeting, where service prioritisation can be linked back to key council values. This is the real test of Best Value: linking finance, resource and outcomes. The aspiration, according to the Task Force, should be a system of three-year rolling budgets, and this is planned to emerge from the

Comprehensive Spending Review. At present, uncertainty over future year grants and council tax capping limits dominate strategic budgetary processes. The aspiration of the Task Force is that policy-led budgeting be implemented for budget setting from 1999/2000. All departments by that time should be able to prepare service plans on a three-year basis subject to the availability of three-year budget plans.

IMPLEMENTATION

The Task Force which outlined these essential elements of Best Value was made up of four representatives from COSLA, three Scottish Office civil servants and a representative from the Accounts Commission. To reinforce the Best Value message, the Scottish Office, in partnership with COSLA and the Accounts Commission, undertook a series of workshops to clarify areas of ambiguity and promote understanding and discussion in advance of first submissions. Council Best Value submissions have been the focus of the Task Force's activity. It has used the submissions to the Task Force to give further guidance to councils, trade unions and direct labour organisations.

The Task Force was handed the remit of developing criteria against which the compliance or otherwise of an authority, as regards Best Value, could be assessed. In terms of guidance, two broad criteria were set by the Secretary of State. Firstly, councils had to complete satisfactorily the various tendering rounds which would have been required had the CCT moratorium not been extended. The second criterion was that councils were asked to indicate how they proposed to demonstrate value for money for 1988 Act services, and how they intended to use competition to generate best value across all council services.

Each council had to make a submission to the Secretary of State for Scotland outlining implementation plans for upgrading systems and processes to meet Best Value criteria . Local authorities were required to give details of the completion of current CCT exercises; self-assessment of Best Value systems and processes currently in place; and documentary evidence to back up the self-assessment. Best Value submissions ranged from three to 1000 pages. In simple terms, at the initial stages, seven councils passed, ten were returned for a little fine-tuning, ten for more work and another five for major re-working. Most councils in their first submissions referred to competition in a very general way and did not set out how they saw its role in the future management of services. In the second wave of submissions a further nine councils passed. Today all 32 councils have gained Scottish Office approval, although special arrangements are in place to monitor developments in Glasgow and West Dumbartonshire.

The Accounts Commission will assess the extent to which councils have implemented their action plans, auditing them to assess the extent to which councils have achieved targets. By the end of 1998 the Scottish Office will receive their report outlining the Accounts Commission assessment of each council's progress. At some point thereafter the Secretary of State will consider then the need for primary legislation.

At present the Task Force is reviewing areas the Secretary of State for Scotland thought required further work. As regards competition, further clarity is needed on how it may best be used. He also asserted that council's performance plans will have to be able to take into account national standards and guidance where relevant. The role of the Scottish Task Force will be to continue to provide advice to councils on the essential elements of the submission to the Secretary of State; continuing the development of the concepts, principles and practices of Best Value; and developing longer term recommendations (Scottish Office/COSLA, 1997).

Best Value is intended to be a process – a long-term drive for better quality and lower costs for all council activities. A further round of self-assessment and a second compliance plan are scheduled for autumn 1998. In the meantime, CCT remains on the statute book even if not activated. In 1999 the Scottish Office will come to a decision on whether, and to what extent, primary legislation is required to formalise Best Value and abolish CCT in its present form.

ASSESSMENT

The Scottish approach contrasts with that in England, where CCT stays in force with only a small minority of local authorities selected as pilots winning a temporary relaxation. The different approach in Scotland reflects contrasting legacies inherited from the 19 years of Conservative government. Over the last two decades the relationship between central government and English local authorities plumbed to depths not experienced in Scotland.

In Scotland the smaller central–local network gives it a degree of intimacy and thus more possibility for consensus to emerge. There is also the fact that in Scotland a stronger public sector ethos in favour of public provision has remained intact, with CCT having far less impact and other policy initiatives such as school opt-outs having almost no impact. There are, however, potential problems and contradictions which require resolution by the Scottish Office.

Firstly, although the talk is of partnership, the Scottish Office retains all the trump cards. The 1994 Local Government etc. (Scotland) Act gives Scottish local authorities, unlike their English counterparts, a statutory responsibility to have in place arrangements for achieving effectiveness, efficiency and economy – central to Best Value. In legal terms, the Secretary of State for Scotland can utilise Section 211 of 1973 Local Government (Scotland) Act which would give him sweeping powers to intervene if he deemed a local council was not delivering Best Value.

Secondly, we noted earlier that Best Value drew on existing managerialist concepts rather than providing a new management agenda. In essence, it is an attempt to formalise a rational planning, participatory and evaluation approach to the management of local government. It would be foolish to ignore the well-recognised limitations of techniques of objective-setting, budgeting and performance measurement in practice, in the complex multi-functional world of local government (Dearlove, 1979).

Like corporate planning in the 1970s, it is being introduced in a tight fiscal context. This is reflected in the assumption that Best Value is cost-free. Filkin asserts that 'Best value recognises the services can be improved without more resources ... In short, more value without more expenditure' (Filkin, 1997b: 10). The Scottish Office share this optimistic cost-free assumption. However, if Best Value is to have the fundamental impact on council operations it is supposed to, there should be some recognition of its costs. After all, the corporate management reforms of the 1970s had many similar aspirations to those of Best Value, in particular the aim of instilling a long-term perspective. As Greenwood *et al.* have noted, the short-term constraints of finance hindered attempts at the development of long term planning. Pressures upon resources created conditions hardly conducive to the operation of several groups composed of senior personnel discussing essentially long-term issues (Greenwood *et al.*, 1976).

In addition, there is now a clear danger of performance measurement overload. We now have three systems operating in parallel with: Statutory Performance Indicators (1992); Audit of Management Arrangements (1994); Best Value (1997). Each of these systems operates concurrently, but there are obvious relationships between each and the question must be asked: why are they not feeding into each other? There are areas of overlap and inconsistency. There is a danger that these are treated as separate exercises (McAteer *et al.*, 1998). The Scottish TUC highlight a related problem: 'In some services, notably education and social work, there already exist independent quality assessment and agencies. In these situations it is not necessary to reinvent the wheel for the purpose of Best Value. The existing work and quality assessments of these bodies should be given their full recognition' (STUC, 1997: para. 4.4) The Scottish Office intends to address these issues jointly with COSLA and the Accounts Commission, by developing key performance indicators for major service areas. In the longer term, of course, arrangements for assessment and audit will be a matter for the new Scottish parliament.

In essence, the Scottish approach, with its emphasis on strategic management and performance planning, is reinvented corporate planning, enshrined in government policy. At the moment, the desire to develop a partnership is succeeding in keeping the lid on the simmering tensions which are emerging over budgetary constraints. The recognition that the government's vision of broad democracy does not yet extend to returning full fiscal autonomy to local government has surprised some, who had been less vocal in their criticism of this year's financial settlement than they would have been had the Conservatives remained in office. Best Value's best hope is that it has emerged from within London local government circles and has been adopted fairly cautiously in recognition of the constraints on such managerial approaches. If the ultimate aim is a self-assessing system with external validation, where every council is demonstrably following or actively seeking Best Value but retaining local choice, it may survive, but it is not in our view a solution to the problems of delivering local services. There is good evidence that the resource problems are more fundamental and, as yet, these remain unaddressed (Carmichael and Midwinter, 1998).

Moreover, performance assessment remains particularly problematic, when based on national studies of value-for-money. A good example of the inherent difficulties can be found in the recent Accounts Commission report on council tax collection, which utilised benchmarking techniques to provide targets for improvement for Scottish councils (Accounts Commission, 1998). On this basis, it concluded that if each council was to achieve the collection rate of their benchmark authorities, then an additional £43 million would be collected in the year it falls due. The report determines the benchmark authorities on the basis of authorities' degree of social deprivation and urbanisation. Although there is clear evidence of a deprivation effect, the report contains no empirical evidence of any urban effect. As these factors are combined to determine family groupings, this undermines the remainder of the analysis.

The report then assumes that the variance between councils and their benchmark is due to less efficient collection, and again offers no evidence to support this. This provides no sound basis for setting judgements over the scope for improvement. As one local authority official told us, 'this does not bode well for Best Value!' Indeed, it raises serious doubts of the notion of the Accounts Commission as 'coach' and the Scottish Office as 'referee' in the game of Best Value. The 'teams' – Scotland's 32 local authorities – have a right to expect Best Value from the coach before the referee can make informed decisions.

Tensions in the partnership approach arose in June 1998, when stories broke in the media of a handful of Scottish Direct Labour Organisations incurring financial deficits of between £3 and £5 million. The Scottish Office immediately took action, serving notice on the authorities, requiring them to explain those losses. Stories of high-earning workers were given prominent coverage by the Scottish press. The Audit Commission was asked to conduct a full audit of all DLOs.

The national language of Best Value gave way to direction and control. The Scottish Secretary began attacking 'in-house provision' (*Herald*, 4 June 1998), whilst the Task Force was stressing that 'What matters is what works. What we are looking for is for local authorities to ensure cost-effective, good quality services. It is not relative to us whether that service is provided in-house or out-house' (*Scotsman*, 3 June 1998).

The Secretary of State has in effect compelled two councils to reconsider their DLO arrangements and put work out to tender. It could be argued this was an over-reaction as most DLOs are not in deficit, have reduced staffing costs in recent years, and have returned services under direct control (Midwinter, 1998). We believe the government may be heading for open conflict with councils and unions over the issue. Councils went to considerable lengths with union support to retain these seervices in-house, whilst Labour in opposition argued it had made serious commitments to rebuild and strengthen locally delivered front-line services and suggested they would work together with councils to deliver them. Recently Unison argued that Scottish local government has never been agnostic on the question of service delivery, and remains hostile to privatisation. It argued that the Scottish Office should drop the thinly veiled threats to restore CCT as it was a discredited and inefficient policy (UNISON, 1998). Best Value, therefore, remains on trial. The problem of such centrally driven managerialist approaches is the gap between planning and implementation. No sooner had East Ayrshire been praised by the Scottish Office for its 'business excellence' than news of its financial deficit discredited that view.

We remain unconvinced of the need for such a centralist approach, which is consistent with the government's general approach to local democracy, of giving direction over governance, service delivery and reducing control of finance. This limited vision is a recipe for conflict, albeit driven by a managerialist ideology rather than the market ideology of the Conservatives.

CONCLUSIONS

The Scottish approach to Best Value has been developed in partnership between central and local government, with some in local councils positively supporting the concept, and others pragmatically recognising the need to play by the new rules of the game. The key concepts are not new but are more formally endorsed by ministers.

At the moment the Scottish Office is about to consult on the development of Best Value indicators. This will take the Accounts Commission performance indicators package as the base and will add 20–30 indicators of output and quality. After the consultation process, the next stage will be the development of forecast targets with an emphasis on 'aspiration', together with 'pragmatism'.

The real test of the success of a policy innovation, however, is if it survives a change of government. In Scotland, that may change after the elections to the new parliament next year. Best Value will survive if councils find it of real value, and if the new government does not alter the rules of the game again.

REFERENCES

Accounts Commission, 1998, *Council Tax Collection* (Edinburgh).
Angus Council, 1997, *Best Value Submission* (Angus Council).
Association of Direct Labour Organisations, 1998, *Direct News* (June).
Biggs, S. and P.Dunleavy, 1995, 'Changing Organisational Forms: a Bureau-Shaping Analysis', in J. Lovenduski and J. Stanyer (eds.), *Contemporary Political Studies*, Vol II (PSA).
Blair, A., 1997, *Leading The Way: A New Vision for Local Government* (London: Institute of Public Policy Research).
Carmichael, P. and A. Midwinter, 1998, 'Downsizing Metropolitan Government in Scotland' (paper presented at Urban Affairs Conference, Houston, Texas, April).
Dearlove, J., 1979, *The Reorganisation of British Local Government* (Cambridge: Cambridge University Press).
Filkin, G., 1997a, 'Best Value for the Public', *Municipal Journal* (Barony Consulting/Solace).
Filkin, G., 1997b, *Political Leadership and Best Value* (ELGIU).
Greenwood, R. *et al.*, 1997, *In Pursuit of Corporate Rationality* (Birmingham: INLOGOV).
Labour Party, *New Labour, Because Britain Deserves Better* (Labour Party).
McAteer, M., C. Mair and K. Orr, 1998, 'The Manager in Local Government: Performance and Best Value' (unpublished lecture, Glasgow: Scottish Local Authorities Management Centre).
Midwinter, A., 1995, *Local Government in Scotland* (Basingstoke: MacMillan).
Midwinter, A., 1998, *Local Government Finance in Scotland* (UNISON).
Pollitt, C., 1986, 'Beyond the Managerial Model: The Case for Broadening Performance Assessment in Government and the Public Services', *Financial Accountability and Management*, Vol.12, No.3, pp.155–70.
Pollitt, C., 1990, *Managerialism and the Public Service: The Anglo American Experience* (Oxford: Blackwell 2nd edn.).
Rees, J., 1996, 'The Case for a Voluntary Regime', *Local Government Chronicle Public Sector PLC* (LGC).
Scottish Local Government Information Unit, 1997, *Best Value Special Issue* (SLGIU).
Scottish Office/COSLA, 1997, Best Value Task Force, *Report to the Secretary of State and Cosla* (Edinburgh)
Scottish Trade Unions Congress, 1997, *Best Value and Competition Issues in Scottish Local Government* (STUC).
Society of Local Authority Chief Executives (Scottish Branch), 1994, *The New Management Agenda* (SOLACE).
Unison Scotland, 1998, *The Future for Scottish Local Government: Local Democracy at Stake?* (Unison).
Walsh, K., 1995, *Public Services and Market Mechanisms* (Basingstoke: MacMillan).

Preparing for Best Value

DEAN BARTLETT, PAUL CORRIGAN,
PAULINE DIBBEN, SIMON FRANKLIN,
PAUL JOYCE, TONY McNULTY
and AIDAN ROSE

Best Value marks a strategic shift in local government policy making. This paper analyses how two local authorities prepared its implementation. CCT aimed to make authorities more innovative but failed because it was highly prescriptive. Best Value provides the opportunity for authorities to make more strategic choices. The two case studies show evidence of greater partnership development and examples of political and technical implementation problems. The paper also analyses opportunities for organisational learning and the role of members and the public. Best Value is seen as an incomplete idea and therefore has the possibility of resulting in a new form of bureaucratisation. Alternatively, if the focus is on community problems then it may enable authorities to be more innovative and dynamic.

In this paper we use case study data from two local authorities to examine how Best Value arrangements are emerging, how the process of introducing change is being handled, how the politicians' and public's roles are being affected by it, and, thus, how competitive forces, internal decision-making processes and public accountability are being articulated through this major innovation in local government.

The first section of the paper presents the Best Value policy and relates it to CCT. Then data is presented on two local authorities which are attempting to pilot Best Value in radically different ways. The analysis emphasises the sequencing of developments to implement Best Value and the fluidity of the situation created by the way in which Best Value has been launched. Finally, the Best Value innovation is placed in perspective by

Dean Bartlett, Paul Corrigan, Pauline Dibben, Simon Franklin, Paul Joyce, Tony McNulty and Aidan Rose, University of North London looking at how the general conditions for innovation are being changed as a result of this policy.

The overall conclusion is that Best Value has created a new strategic direction for the whole of UK local government, that the initial confusion and uncertainty about the most effective paths for moving in this direction are productive rather than barriers to change, and that there are promising signs of local government managers developing an intent to learn from each other and to take advantage of opportunities for partnerships. Of course, we recognise that strategic changes are almost always difficult to implement (Bryson, 1995). Best Value, which is an agenda for improving local government and not an accomplished fact, requires local government to confront the confusions and uncertainties, develop new core competencies in learning and working in partnership, and embed Best Value in a revitalised democratic relationship to the public and a vigorous responsiveness to the service user. If it succeeds in these matters, it will have found a third way – neither bureaucracy nor the market – based on a regime of local accountability which both subordinates and uses bureaucracy and competitive forces for meeting community and user needs.

EVALUATING BEST VALUE

Local government has been pressurised by political changes over the last two decades. Central–local relations over the last 20 years have been typically described as adversarial. Conflict often led to legal battles with the use of punitive sanctions. However, it would be a mistake to see the national political system as the only agent for change in the environment of local government (Caulfield and Schultz, 1993), and equally it would be a mistake to see the past pattern of adverserial central–local relations as continuing. The work so far on best value, coming as it does prior to legislation, is one piece of evidence of the relationship being recast along the lines of partnership, even if this is based on an understanding that if local authorities fail to deliver, then, according to the Prime Minister, central government will look to other partners. A key player in this new relationship, albeit in the last chance saloon, is the Local Government Association, who have set up new co-operative relationships with local government trade unions and others in pursuit of Best Value. Perhaps the most positive indicator is that 150 authorities were prepared to submit Best Value bids within a tightly limited time-frame. This involved the identification of an acknowledged weakness in the local authority together with a programme for remedying that weakness. The Hawthorne effect is well known to organisation theorists. Few of the prophets of doom during the 1980s would have predicted that so many authorities would have sought the gaze of government and their researchers over their Achilles' heel. One danger is that the enthusiasm of the 110 authorities not selected for pilot status will be lost. Networks within the local government movement are afoot to capture this energy.

A second area of optimism is based on the messages emerging from the pilot application process. Many of the applications address long-standing local government problems, many of which were exacerbated during the 1980s and 1990s. Many proposals aim to overcome departmental boundaries, to experiment with corporate processes or to address problems which do not have traditional departmental 'homes'. Thus, one of the weaknesses of the so-called 'new public management' is addressed. The disaggregation of organisations into their constituent units has created a chimney-stack mentality where success factors related to the unit of production rather than the output or the outcome of the service process. Issues such as networking and the interconnectedness of local government activities are back on the agenda. Here, perhaps are the seeds of a new approach to local government which is prepared to learn how to make better policy and to construct better, more informed relations with users. The real answers are not likely to be available in the short term. It would be careless of government to pick 40 pilots from 150 without being sure that the large majority are capable of meeting unspecified success criteria.

Data was gathered from one shire district council and one metropolitan district council. Interviews were conducted at chief executive level and with policy officers and service managers together with service users. In addition, a focus group was conducted with all those interviewed in attendance. Data was analysed using NUD-IST. Best Value is a strategic shift in local government policy making. Consequently, its implementation offers a valuable opportunity to examine how local authorities are addressing and re-addressing policy and managerial arrangements under a new government. A number of aspects of Best Value are of interest. First, we seek to analyse the impact of the change from compulsory competitive tendering and the increased emphasis placed on performance measurement and the experimentation with new techniques including benchmarking. Second, we seek to examine the way in which the selected authorities developed partnerships with organisations in the public, private and voluntary sectors. Third, we discussed the implementation problems that authorities are facing. Fourth, the roles of politicians and the public in developing best value proposals are discussed. Finally, given the move away from the prescriptive regime imposed by compulsory competitive tendering, we are interested in the capacity of the authorities for innovation.

THE SOUTH-EAST COUNCIL

The south-east council has a reputation for being innovative. For example, it was one of a number of councils that had experimented with community planning. Internally, it has a management culture of taking responsibility, delegation and project working. The bid to be a Best Value pilot was seen by one interviewee in the following way: 'the submission of the bid was a project and people are pulled from different parts of the organisation to work on different elements of it, and bring it all together.'

In common with many authorities piloting Best Value, it was recorded that the bid was building on work already under way in the authority. Whilst there was no user consultation in preparing the pilot bid, there was informal internal marketing of the bid in the south-east council. The Best Value bid was said to have been built around what the council already did and that was how it was promoted: 'certainly the message that we're trying to get across is that ... don't look upon this as something that's totally radical and totally new and everything else, because we're already doing a lot of it.' As explained by the chief executive, however, the difference was that they would 'lock together' all the things they had been doing.

The south-east council had set up a system – comprising organisational arrangements and procedures – for introducing and operationalising Best Value. The council had a Best Value working group which met fortnightly and a members' Best Value group which met monthly. They also had an advisory panel, including representatives of outside groups and they assigned responsibility for key elements of Best Value to particular individuals. One manager was made responsible for consultation under Best Value. At the time of interviewing, this person was gathering information from all service managers in the council as a prelude to developing a corporate approach to consultation by co-ordinating and standardising such activities. The procedural aspect of the new system was based on a review schedule which was designed to take managers through each of the different constituent parts of the review process. The service managers who were to be affected by the first wave of Best Value reviews were being asked to specify how the review will take place, the timetable, who they will consult, and so on.

There was still a lot of confusion within the south-east council about the nature of Best Value. One interviewee identified this as a problem: 'There has been a tendency for some people to move very quickly whereas still there's quite a lot of the organisation are still sort of thinking, well you know, what's Best Value? What is it all about?' The chief executive seemed to think that it was the council's and the government's fault that not many staff understood what Best Value was. They had used newsletters and other methods to inform people – but 'Best Value is something that nobody really knew what it was, including the government'. This last point is of interest partly because it suggests that there could be no authoritative source of the meaning of Best Value, and partly because the lack of a definition to be imposed by government creates wider possibilities of ownership of the Best Value concept. Local authorities will be making the meaning of Best Value for themselves, and in making it they have a relationship of ownership.

THE NORTH OF ENGLAND COUNCIL

This local authority had enjoyed a period of being in the public spotlight during the 1980s but was described by one interviewee as 'being a bit stuck in the mud'. Nevertheless, the council submitted a proposal to be a Best Value pilot, offering to pilot Best Value on an issue which had emerged as one of five priorities in its community plan. This issue was a matter of concern in the local community – and not a service delivery problem as such. The issue appears to have been chosen because it was felt to be a 'wicked issue' and it also fitted in with forthcoming statutory requirements. In consequence, the bid encompassed a number of different areas of service delivery which it were felt might make particular contributions to the tackling of the issue.

The Community Plan had been developed in January 1997 and had been based on major attempts at consultation with the public. The consultation channels included a special questionnaire sent to thousands of households; panels and forums which attracted over 6,000 people annually; and a standing survey panel of 2,500 operated with other local partners.

The pilot bid was drafted between July and September 1997 by a corporate group of officers. They identified the issue, called together a group of officers from around all the directorates and service areas in the council. These officers were asked to go back into their service areas and then to come back with suggestions and ideas about which services might contribute to addressing the aim. This led to a number of specific services being included in the bid. Approval for these proposals was then secured through the internal decision-making structures of the council. First the bid went to the Management Board, then it went to the Council's Policy Board, which is the joint meeting of the Management Board and the leadership team of members. The Policy Board gave its support to the bid and the bid's proposals. It was then fed into the committee cycle to get formal member approval and backing. However, it should be noted that processing of the bid was quite demanding in the relatively short time scale covering the month of August, when the committee cycle was suspended.

It may be noted, therefore, that the bidding process to become a Best Value pilot was officer-led with member support in the form of a 'rubber-stamping' exercise. There is little evidence of public involvement in the critical period of drafting and finalising the bid. Nor is there much evidence that local partners played a role in the drawing up the Best Value bid.

THE REVIEW PROCEDURES AND BENCHMARKING

The green paper on Best Value (DETR, 1998) clearly indicates that performance measurement systems are at the heart of the Best Value process. Authorities are urged to develop and refine methodologies for measuring performance, with increased emphasis on outputs and outcomes. This is linked with an emerging interest in benchmarking as a technique for comparing service performance with that of other organisations. Our evidence shows that authorities recognise that they are at the early stages of this process and there remains much work to be done.

At the time of our interviewing, in early 1998, some of the managers in south-east council seemed to be thinking that CCT generally, and the manager's role in the tendering process especially, were not evolving so much as being replaced by review procedures and benchmarking. One officer told us: 'I think with Best Value there will be some paperwork because obviously you do have to have a specification of the service to be able to benchmark so you make sure you're comparing another authority service like with like.' At times it sounded as if managers were confused about the retention of a role in CCT, but still tended to think of the change in terms of a replacement for a role in tendering by a new role in benchmarking. One officer commented on the implications for job content:

> Certainly my job will change, and I think a lot of people's jobs will change, because we will be exempt from CCT as a result of Best Value. So my role as far as CCT will not cease but there will be no need to do monitoring that I do now and the contract checks and all the rest of it. That role will cease and it will be replaced with a Best Value role. The feedback I've got so far is that we need to be, I need to be, looking at benchmarking and setting up some benchmarking groups. And that type of thing.

Interviews revealed that many managers were tending to think of benchmarking with other local authorities rather than the private sector. Was this because it would be easier to share information with other local authorities, or was it because Best Value was seen as enabling local authorities to justify their activities rather than compete with the private sector to provide local services? Some of the remarks made in interviews suggested a shift to a process of justifying service delivery decisions, and consulting the public on those decisions, rather than a review process in which options were appraised and the best option selected on the basis of a prior determination of the public's needs.

At the same time, there were those who considered Best Value to be something they were doing already: 'our bid for Best Value essentially is built around what we already do. It's interesting that some of the things we're already doing are actually now starting to feature in initiatives such as Best Value which perhaps other authorities see as being new or different. But to us, we're already doing it.'

At the northern council, managers had been developing methods of performance monitoring and felt that this would be helped along by Best Value. Review arrangements under Best Value were seen as consolidating performance management systems. The bid submitted by the council had outlined a number of performance indicators, targets and consultation mechanisms. The setting of targets and performance indicators to measure effectiveness and quality had not been fully developed. We were told: 'we're very much on the starting blocks for that one, and I wouldn't want to say at this point in time what we can and can't achieve because we just don't know.'

The details of how the review procedures would be operated were still unclear in some respects. For example, benchmarking was mentioned as perhaps being important in the northern council as a way of demonstrating Best Value. This, it was pointed out, meant that some services would be facing bench-marking in comparison to the private sector. Additionally it was mentioned that confusion may arise as local authorities struggle to find adequate comparator services or agencies in the market against which to compare performance.

PARTNERS

Leadbeatter and Goss (1998) point to the importance of working across boundaries as a way of brokering access to resources, ideas and expertise. Several initiatives involving local government including community care and the Single Regeneration Budget have sought to encourage this. Best Value continues this focus by encouraging links with other organisations in all sectors and service users. Best Value could be seen as encouraging a governance model of public service delivery. Rhodes defines governance as 'self-organising networks' with 'complex sets of organisations drawn from the public and private sectors' (1996: 658).

We were told by the chief executive at the south-east council: 'We'll build partnerships with anybody ... we only survive through partnerships and developments towards a network forum.' At the northern council the early phases of preparing for Best Value had not involved much work on partnerships. There had been little progress in deciding and agreeing how partnerships will operate in order to ensure the effective implementation of the Best Value pilot. The authority intended to develop its relationships with a range of current partnerships, but it appeared that the work to develop them had been patchy. What work had been done took the form of initial liaison meetings and tentative development of plans of action. In some areas of service delivery covered by the bid there were established partnership relations which it was felt could be effectively utilised, whereas, in other areas, Best Value partnerships were in their infancy. The effectiveness of partnership relations have been variable in the past – with some being constructive and effective, and others not always being so productive. For example, it was suggested that 'in some areas of Social Services, relations with the Police and NHS Trusts can be a bit up and down, whereas relations with probation services, neighbouring authorities and the Health Authority have always been good and constructive'. One interviewee told us: 'we need to do quite a lot to improve liaison, … and there's an awful lot of work to do there. How that will all fit together we don't know yet.' There had been little progress at all in developing relations with the private sector. We were told: 'one of the things that we haven't really looked at too closely yet in this process is our relationship with the private sector.'

IMPLEMENTATION PROBLEMS

Implementation problems encountered in the very early phase of developing Best Value take two principal forms: political and technical. By political problems we mean that the Best Value concept, or the way it was being introduced, was not acceptable to some of the coalitions within the local authority.

In the south-east council some problems were evident in the reaction of elected members and staff. It seems that initially the Labour politicians had been disappointed as they had anticipated greater financial freedom from the Labour government. The staff reaction was to worry about streamlining. There was also evidence of friction between elected members and officers. One elected member, for example, described Best Value as about the provision of services within tight financial restraints, keeping members and officers 'on their toes', and the involvement of the people. Expressed in this way, the immediate reaction of staff might be to feel that government pressure for more efficiency would continue to bear down upon them whilst also requiring that they become more answerable to the public.

The chief executive reported that there had been resistance to Best Value by service managers: 'the most important thing was to convince those managers what was best value about, if not convince them, to inform them.

And it was difficult to start with because there was a cloak of, why have we been selected? ... Is it because we're poor performers?' This raises a potential problem for service managers in local authorities.

In the northern council it was evident that political problems could arise from the new demands placed on those involved in its implementation. Best Value was felt to be causing pressure and stress. There were concerns that coping with Best Value work might deflect attention from other prioritised work. It was stated that it was essential that those who have to implement Best Value on the ground are not overloaded, and that there was no guarantee this would happen. One interviewee said: 'can you actually do everything well, and can we still maintain our focus on doing the other things that need doing irrespective of Best Value ... because if you're involved in Best Value ... you're having to prepare so many other things ... and that time is taken from actually getting on with doing other things that we want to do. So there's the pressure.' It appears that key front-line staff do not at present have any knowledge about how performance planning arrangements will be put into practice. Nor, it was said, had they engaged in any preliminary work or discussions. Consequently, some of the political problems of implementation might be overcome if the involvement and consultation of staff is deepened as the pilot activity proceeds.

Technical problems are centred on lack of knowledge about how the idea of Best Value could be best realised in practice. There appeared to be technical problems in the northern council. There was a lack of knowledge about how the benchmarking could be done in some cases: 'if we're being asked at the end of the day to demonstrate Best Value, then some of the services it will be very difficult to compare with other services. For some of them, there aren't people in the market to test against.'

CULTURE SHIFT: OPENNESS, LEARNING AND OUTCOMES

Best Value is one of several initiatives which the Labour government is introducing and should be seen in the overall context of developing new sets of relationships. Other initiatives include democratic renewal and a reconsideration of the ethical agenda. Taken together, there is a renewed focus on culture in and around local government, stressing the need for authorities to be more outward-looking and community focused.

At least one of our interviewees in the northern council considered that Best Value would entail a big culture shift for both the elected members and the council's officers. In the south-east council we were informed by one manager that the ending of CCT could bring about more openness through sharing of information. This was, according to one manager, partly because, under CCT, people had been frightened about giving information in case it fell into the hands of contractors. It was also partly because Best Value entailed benchmarking.

As well as more open information, the new culture could be one of more openness to learning. According to one northern council interviewee, this learning is being sought with and from others: 'I mean we're particularly keen to be part of the learning process of the Best Value pilot and to share with other authorities, both within the pilots and external to it ... we're keen to share information, learn from others and have others learn from us.'

If learning does become a more dominant motif in local government culture, we could see this supporting a community leadership role. Asquith argues that local authorities are moving towards a community leadership role – some faster than others – and that those in this role are those with the most effective strategies for proactive local government (Asquith, 1997: 90). Interviewees at the south-east council saw authorities becoming more concerned with community issues and thought this would have an impact on the nature of the organisation: 'One of the interesting things that is starting to come through now as far as local authorities is concerned is this idea of the major themes, major issues, and the way the authority deals with these is almost as if the organisation has to be a lot more fluid.' Leach *et al.* (1994) discuss the implications of community-enabling for organisational form. They argue that principles of internal organisation include matrix management, decentralisation and inter-professional co-operation. Community issues require problem solving rather than simple service delivery, and that requires a move away from rigidity in organisational form.

Another aspect of the culture shift appears to be learning how to focus local government on outcomes rather than outputs. In the case of the northern council, the Best Value approach is being applied to a community issue which will be addressed through a co-ordinated approach with other local partners. In practical terms, this means coping intellectually and emotionally with the need to achieve results in outcomes that matter to the community, rather than service outputs which are more controllable by producers of services. Managers at the northern council were struggling to place this within a performance management framework:

> as yet we have not formulated these ... it's incredibly difficult isn't it in terms of actually saying "Is what we have done in these initiatives responsible for benefits" – you know, proving cause and effect links as we know is very difficult ... we have looked at an issue rather than a particular service or whatever, and in an area where there are no predetermined measurement factors if you like. So I think we're conscious of, as yet, we have yet to develop what success criteria we're going to have for this scheme.

THE POLITICIANS' ROLE IN BEST VALUE

In Leach *et al.*'s community enabling model there is a strong role for elected members. They argue that under such a model there would be 'relatively strong strategic and policy-making roles for elected members to provide a framework for local choice' (1994: 249). At the heart of this role is the need for members to be involved in the identification of community needs. At the same time, there is increased emphasis on the gathering of data about community and user needs through, for example, surveys. Hence, there may be sources of data about needs alternative to those obtained through traditional methods of community representation and accountability.

There was little evidence from the northern council case study that Labour members, who formed the majority party on the council, were providing the leadership for the Best Value innovation. No flag-wavers or sponsors from the Labour Group were visible. Our data does not reveal the causes for this situation. It was not clear, for example, if other aspects of the Labour government's reform agenda were more interesting to the politicians than the Best Value policy. Nor was it clear from the data whether their attention was mainly directed to council committee work or responsibilities or to electoral and party political matters locally.

Attitudes towards Best Value amongst elected members seemed to be broadly positive, though there was some concern that Best Value may not replace CCT. We found, for instance, a preference for Best Value over CCT because it was Labour's version of CCT; we found a view that it would help to keep up pressure for service improvements; and we heard that it was bringing the virtues of in-house provision and the ethos of public service back on to the local government stage.

THE PUBLIC'S ROLE IN BEST VALUE

Leadbetter and Goss suggest 'public sector organisations that wish to develop new services often need to innovate with new, often informal, ways to negotiate consent, through user forums, panels and conferences (1998: 55). At the time of the fieldwork which was conducted in early 1998, the south-east council was considering developing neighbourhood forums, more surveys and a citizens' panel. It might also employ new techniques, including user and service panels to test particular services.

At the northern council the approach to local accountability was being developed through existing community consultative mechanisms, meaning that accountability would be citizen-led rather than user-led. It appeared to be assumed that the community consultation they had done adequately reflected the views of service users. At present there appears to be little planning for accountability mechanisms which could demonstrate Best Value to users of actual services. A firm commitment to developing greater accountability focused on newsletters, providing users with more information. There did not appear to be a sophisticated body of knowledge about how two-way interactions with the public might work. As one interviewee commented, 'something that we should be doing is looking at ways of gathering views from users covered by the services within the bid'.

Best Value's potential for opening up the local authority to a closer relationship with the public might be obvious further down the line of implementation. Certainly there were indications that northern council interviewees could see some issues which would need attention. For example, there was a concern that Best Value will make apparent the fact that local government provision is more expensive than private sector provision, but might not enable the reasons to become more explicit. There was another concern that the accountability arrangements might not be transparent enough to prevent a build-up of unrealisable public expectations. Both these types of issue would obviously threaten local government unless Best Value led to further opening up by councils.

The idea that there was a new deal for the public emerging from Best Value and that the council would have to be proactive and put things on a new footing can be seen in the following comments by one of our interviewees: 'I think as far as the community is concerned too, they've got to be won over to the fact that there is a genuine commitment to actually change practices that they've been used to for so long, and that this is actually a real initiative if you like.'

INNOVATION AND BEST VALUE

At the moment there is a very clear contrast in the form of change. CCT was implemented through considerable detail of legislation and regulation; best value is taking place largely outside of legislation. Is Best Value an evolution of CCT – or is it displacing CCT? This will take years, not months, of implementing Best Value to answer. But, in the long run, the question provides one way of making sense of the nature of Best Value. If Best Value is pragmatically driven by competitive tendering, then it will have been an evolution from CCT. If Best Value ever comes to be seen as primarily driven by benchmarking, whether it is based on benchmarking against private sector or local government providers, then we could see competitive rivalry spur higher levels of public service performance, even though services are not necessarily put out to competitive tender. In both cases, it could be argued that competition has been harnessed for public services. But if Best Value becomes largely a review process used to justify in-house service providers then it will have displaced CCT by eliminating tendering as a competitive tool. Of course, there are other possible outcomes too.

The spirit of Best Value may be side-stepped by the bureaucratic routines adopted for its implementation, but only if during implementation the politicians and the public fail to engage with the review process. If it becomes bureaucratised and is not placed within a democratic framework and made locally accountable to service users, we can expect a number of bureaucratic symptoms to appear. First, councils will try and construct a review process that they can entirely control, which means that they hope they will be able to fix the outcomes of the review process. Second, they will try to diminish the uncertainty of competition. This will mean avoiding competitive tendering even if it produces better value for the public. It will mean selectivity in benchmarking – retreating into closed and protected benchmarking within the local government sector and the avoidance of benchmarking against the private sector. Finally, bureaucratisation might show up in attempts by councils to put themselves into situations where they feel their performance and results cannot easily be measured and compared because they are addressing very specific local issues which do not throw up very obvious comparators. This last bureaucratic symptom would turn local differentiation into a device to close off public accountability rather than a tool of adapting the council to meet local community needs.

Best Value has been deliberately offered to local government as an uncompleted idea so that it can be developed and applied by local government itself. This means that implementation is intentionally a fluid experience with many local variations in how Best Value is being defined and with the possibility of councils evolving and modifying what it means as they go along. Therefore, it is quite possible, in making use of the concept of Best Value, and in applying it, local government may take itself on a pathfinding route which embraces openness to the public, and uncertainty. Alternatively, local government may seek to turn the clock back in search of a more comfortable, because insulated, situation. If the latter route is taken then councils will compete only in the race to appear innovative and progressive – to be seen to be doing well rather than actually doing well. Best Value will then not be a 'real initiative', as one of our interviewees commented.

One of our case studies is a pilot where outputs and outcomes are being sought in relation to community problems rather than council service delivery. This means that the council has volunteered to deal with the far more uncertain activities of community leadership and community achievement rather than with the easier issues of service delivery and council achievement. The council has chose to co-ordinate a whole series of services in a concerted effort to address the community problem. They have sought agreement also to co-ordinate their efforts with local partners. This has made the task of creating Best Value much more technically complex. There may be some confusion between the outcome of the whole thing and the outcomes of the individual areas of service delivery which make up the co-ordinated effort. They are answering through their pilot the question of how a council evaluates something that is not clearly direct service delivery but is instead a problem-solving and partnership process. This places innovation now within an inter-organisational dynamic – which is far more ambitious than innovations within a single service provider unit.

The implications of this for innovation in local government would appear to be that the prospects for innovation will depend on a number of factors. These include the choice made between openness to the public, partnerships, experimentation and uncertainty or bureaucratic control and the search for an insulation from competition and the public.

Relationships within local authorities will be very important for the implementation of Best Value. It is evident from our case study work that there is now a generation of officers who have worked within a CCT culture and who have now been challenged to think differently. This can be termed a cultural issue. In particular, under CCT many managers developed an expertise in 'getting round' legislative requirements. Best Value does not offer the same kind of target for this expertise as CCT did. There is nothing to 'get round' until local government has created it. The widespread confusion about what it is and the uncertainty about how it can be made to work suggests both a realisation that there is a new posture from central government and an initial desire to engage with Best Value to make it work. For this reason there may be a genuine impetus towards the creativity and proactivity needed for innovation.

The managers at the centre of councils will have an important role to play in fostering creativity and proactivity. Best Value offers an opportunity for the centre to own the process of review and demonstrate their superiority as champions of innovation over their service manager counterparts. It gives, for example, policy functionalists a whole new world in which to play, and to make service directors take action. The policy functionalists will have power on a par with the Department of Environment in the old relationship between central and local government. 'Regulations' could flow from the policy heads to the service departments, and the service departments will then have to discover ways of 'getting round' them.

Perhaps we could end up with everybody working at cross-purposes. Councillors might try to 'bash' their officers with Best Value. The centre might use it as the latest demonstration of its own importance. Service managers protesting about the pressure and the strain involved might dismiss Best Value as yet another gimmick; and the front-line staff might complain that nobody tells them anything. However, there is also the possibility – as a result of the way Best Value has been introduced – that these different stakeholders will see in it a general plan for what needs to be done and how it needs to be done. Moreover, it may be assumed that many of the people concerned will feel that it is broadly in accord with democratic ideas of serving the public and a more humane way of managing competition than CCT. It is striking that in spring 1997 no one knew Best Value existed, yet one year later there were people in local authorities claiming that they are doing it already. The implementation of Best Value is far from a mechanistic process. The case studies found evidence of hesitation and uncertainty. They provide a snapshot of fluidity, and that itself is interesting in a process of change. Of course, the intention in using pilots was to find ways of retaining fluidity.

CONCLUSIONS

CCT was brought in as a tool for innovation. However, it denied local authorities the possibility of acting outside very tight regulations. It was therefore an attempt at innovation that denied local innovation. It succeeded in enforcing change and within this straightjacket created its own form of innovation. Direct service organisations had to innovate in a number of ways in relation to CCT – in working methods, training, equipment, style of management, relations with unions – all of which were to do with the process of service delivery. Whilst elected members and managers fashioned strategic intents, corporate values and strategies, and business plans to handle CCT, they were not able to set strategic directions to steer these service improvements and innovations.

We do not know whether Best Value will lead to more or less innovation; all we do know is that it represents a different set of conditions. Managers experience these as conditions of uncertainty. Staff on the front-line and in the service areas experience these conditions as another set of regulations, and therefore as a similar experience to CCT. However, Best Value can be used by the elected politicians and managers to create a new set of experiences for employees, partners and the public which may educate all the stakeholders so that they can benefit from newer experiences around innovation in service delivery and possibly community problem solving.

We must reiterate here the fact that the case study data presented above shows two councils concentrating on the first wave of work involved in creating their own Best Value models. At this point they were concentrating on forming their systems of review, benchmarking and performance management. The fact that other aspects of the Best Value agenda were not prominent in our case studies does not mean that they will be missing when more work has been done. The most important focus at present is for local authorities to develop appropriate review systems.

We can also make the point on the basis of our two case studies that Best Value is taking very different forms, with radically different conceptions about who is to benefit. In one case the beneficiaries of Best Value are service users. In the other case the concept of service users is much more complex because it depends which services – provided by the council and by other agencies – are brought into a co-ordinated response – co-alignment – to address a community problem. The two cases reveal the fact that local government activity can either be a straightforward activity of trying to get service delivery right or it can be about trying to do something for the local community. In the latter case, the council is going to have to measure its performance – as will their partner agencies which are also public services. This will take persistence and creativity to develop the Best Value methodology that is needed.

The case studies have also underlined the way in which public services are coalitions of responsibilities, skills and interests. We have found ourselves thinking about the roles of councillors, service managers, policy specialists, front-line service providers, service users and citizens. All these particular groups are shaping the implementation process of what is becoming Best Value. At the moment there is no one thing which is Best Value; all the people actively engaged in creating Best Value pilots might think they have gone out to do something which is Best Value – but nobody actually knows precisely what it is.

The relationship between Best Value and democratic renewal in local government did not emerge from our case studies as an important issue. This is surprising. The Best Value framework offers a plan for encouraging discussion, service review and consultation with the public. Instead of providers deciding what is best for the public and then delivering it with a take it or leave it attitude, councils will be talking with the public. Instead of relying on competition between providers to create efficiency and innovation, councils will work in partnership with the public to increase efficiency and effectiveness. Surely, such experiences will foster the growth of a democratic capacity which institutional reforms can take advantage of, but not create?

Success can only be evaluated four or five years down the line. However, it is possible to predict two possible fates for the initiative. One possible fate is that Best Value will be a victim of its own success. A new relationship with service users will be created. Strategic decision-making capacities will be enhanced to the extent at which they will be hampered by the centrally imposed review criteria. The second possible fate is that Best

Value will become the new local government industry. Every local authority will have completed, say, eight reviews in year one and the real cost of the process will be realised with little evidence of real improvements. Fewer, wider, slimmer reviews will be required by central government with increasingly centralised performance criteria. Best Value becomes the new routine; no strategic view is developed. Instead, most authorities try to avoid low positions in the league tables and referral to the Secretary of State.

If Best Value is to work, it must be understood as a concept rather than as a fully designed process, let alone a series of isolated events. Key to its success is that the concept and its application is understood at both the officer and member level and that the required recasting of roles is visible and understood by officers. New relationships with the public are going to be problematic. Tools for innovation, such as pilot projects and greater openness, together with a taking on board of the need for inter-connectedness in local governance, are at the heart of the initiative's success.

NOTES

The empirical data for this paper was collected as part of an ESRC project No.L125251044 entitled 'User-Led Innovation in Local Government'.

REFERENCES

Asquith, A., 1997, 'Community Leadership', *Local Government Studies*, Vol.23, No.4, pp.86–99.
Bryson, J.M., 1995, *Strategic Planning for Public and Nonprofit Organizations* (San Francisco, CA: Jossey-Bass, rev. edn.).
Caulfield, I. and J. Schultz, 1993, *Planning for Change: Strategic Planning in Local Government* (Harlow: Longman).
DETR, 1998, *Modernising Local Government: Improving Local Services through Best Value* (London: DETR).
Leach, S., J. Stewart and K. Walsh, 1994, *The Changing Organisation and Management of Local Government* (Basingstoke: Macmillan).
Leadbeatter, C. and S. Goss, 1998, *Civic Entrepreneurship* (London: Demos).
Rhodes, R.A.W., 1996, 'The New Governance: Governing without Government', *Political Studies*, XLIV, pp.652–67.

A Whole-Authority Approach to
Testing and Developing Best Value

D. BRIAN JAMES and JOSEPH J. FIELD

For the Welsh unitaries and some authorities in England, the culture changes required by the Best Value regime have been additional to those accompanying a recent reorganisation of local government. The Best Value pilot studies are being evaluated in England by Warwick University and in Wales by the Cardiff Business School and they are being monitored by external auditors. This work will facilitate a thorough critical review of the process, yet there is much which can also be learned through self analysis by the pilots themselves and by sharing their experiences with others. This paper explains how Torfaen County Borough Council responded to the challenge of Best Value, outlines the corporate approach taken by the authority, and provides a perspective from the head of a service department.

BACKGROUND

Torfaen County Borough Council was established as one of 22 new unitary authorities upon local government reorganisation in Wales in April 1996. The authority comprises a varied 12-mile-long valley from Blaenafon in the north through Pontypool to Cwmbran in the south. The most eastern of Welsh valleys, it is an area of great diversity, with the communities having been originally shaped from the forces of the iron and coal industries. It is also an area of great geographical contrast, with raw, well-beaten landscapes and attractive rolling hills and meadows complementing the areas of industry and commerce. It covers an area of approximately 126 square kilometres and has a population of some 90,700.

On its creation, the new unitary authority, which has a large Labour majority, developed a clear vision supported by a statement of values, which guided its progress and development through local government reorganisation. It agreed a mission statement from the outset in 1996, reflecting the elements of continuous improvement, which now lie at the

Brian James and Joseph Field, Torfaen County Borough

heart of Best Value, namely: 'To Improve the Quality of Life in Torfaen, Significantly and Continuously.' The Council's vision and values emphasise a strong customer focus and the need to represent the aspirations of the people of the area.

Upon local government reorganisation, the authority was required, through the Local Government (Wales) Act 1994, to produce a service delivery plan for its first full year of operation. The main objective of this process was to achieve a seamless transition of services from the pre-reorganisation authorities to the new unitary council. A subsequent study conducted by the District Audit Service judged that the transition had been successful and that the authority had performed to a very high standard in all the major aspects of the reorganisation process. Whilst it was not a statutory duty to produce service delivery plans in subsequent years, the authority made a conscious decision to continue with the process and to maximise the opportunities that this embryonic planning activity offered. By the time the Best Value initiative emerged in the summer of 1997, Torfaen had successfully completed its second service delivery plan and the service planning process had become an integral part of the authority's culture. The process has since continuously developed and the authority's 1999/2000 community service and performance plan includes separate community plans for the three main conurbations within the county borough. These plans highlight the distinct and diverse issues which affect each of these principal communities. The 1999/2000 plan also includes four separate community focus initiatives, which are aimed at addressing specific community safety and community development issues in areas of greatest need.

In addition, the plan examines each aspect of Torfaen life, it reports on the current year's performance against targets as well as the objectives for next year. Finally, the plan details how the council aims to improve performance in each of the 21 service areas reviewed in Phase I of the Best Value evaluation study in 1998.

DEVELOPING THE CONCEPT OF BEST VALUE

The Corporate Commitment

Following the government's announcement of the introduction of the new concept of Best Value (Armstrong, 1997), Torfaen set out to develop a process of staged discussion in order to determine how the initiative should be introduced and developed within the authority.

Firstly, and armed with the original 12 principles of Best Value (Armstrong, 1997) and the report of the Welsh Office's Best Value Project Group (Welsh Office, 1997), the corporate management team and senior managers met for a full day to consider the likely implications of the new initiative. The exercise, which involved presentations and discussion groups, incorporated a review of the authority's previous performance, an assessment of its position at that time, together with an examination of how Best Value could link in to the authority's developing service planning and performance management processes. As a separate exercise, the elected members and corporate management team convened a seminar, again facilitated through presentations and workshops, to look at the strategic implications of Best Value for the authority. The two sessions proved to be invaluable in providing an opportunity to examine the concepts of Best Value, in engendering constructive debate on the key issues and in assessing options for its incorporation within the authority. A strong shared view emerged that Torfaen could provide a distinctive approach to Best Value. It was felt the authority could make a positive contribution to the introduction and development of Best Value within local government generally. It was also considered the authority was well placed to adopt a whole-authority approach for testing the framework in the Wales and DETR evaluation studies.

Organisational Arrangements

In order to take the initiative forward in a purposeful and systematic manner, the council established a Best Value committee, comprising primarily the chairs of the main committees. A Best Value focus group, consisting of a selection of first-tier and second-tier officers from each of the authority's departments, was created for the purpose of managing and implementing the process internally. This group is led by the Director of Contract Services, with the support of the Performance Management and Business Planning Officer. The progress of the focus group is guided and overseen by a senior officer project board, under the direction of the Chief Executive, as illustrated in Fig. 1. The Best Value focus group representatives are responsible, with the support of their departmental management teams, for driving, supporting and monitoring the development of Best Value within their departments. However, the individual directors retain accountability for managing and implementing the initiative in their departments.

The authority recognised at an early stage that Best Value would not succeed without the commitment and support of all staff. To achieve this commitment it was essential to assist staff in gaining a clear understanding of the new concept, to consider how they would be affected by its introduction and to determine their role in contributing to its successful development. An authority-wide cross-departmental diagonal staff and trade union seminar served to explore options for getting the message across. The recommendations arising from this seminar allowed a corporate Best Value communications strategy to be developed for guidance to managers. The strategy incorporated:

- departmental awareness-raising/induction sessions;

- the inclusion of Best Value in all departmental, divisional and sectional management meetings and team briefings;

- its inclusion in all one-to-one performance review discussions (Investors In People);

- its inclusion in departmental newsletters and briefing sheets;

- regular monitoring through further and periodic authority-wide diagonal slice review seminars.

The Strategic Platform

Upon local government reorganisation in Wales in April 1996, Torfaen had developed an integrated authority-wide approach to service planning and to its internal organisational development. The process combined two complementary and inter-related components. The first part, the community and performance plan, enabled the key service stakeholders, through an extensive mechanism of consultation and review, to contribute to formulating the authority's key objectives for the subsequent financial year. The resulting plan essentially becomes the service contract between the authority, its customers and other service stakeholders. The process, which has been reviewed and refined over three annual planning cycles is now well established across all departments. Secondly, the departmental service and organisational development plans are also produced annually and provide details of the key objectives of each department. They outline the methodology for achieving the objectives, focusing specifically on team and individual accountabilities.

Performance Management

The council's performance management strategy was developed to ensure the objectives of the departmental service and organisational development plans are being achieved with the aim of fulfilling the needs of the overall community and performance plan. The strategy involves a range of processes which have already been developed to varying degrees across all departments. They include:

Investors In People: The council has committed itself to the national standard. Considerable progress has already been achieved with seven of the authority's eight departments anticipating formal recognition by early 1999.

Performance Assessment: A performance assessment scheme for chief officers and assistant directors involves agreeing annual objectives with the officers and regularly reviewing their progress. The annual reviews are conducted by the elected members.

Quality Systems: A number of quality initiatives are being tested and incorporated into different parts of the organisation. These include ISO 9000, Charter Mark and EFQM.

Service Level Agreements: The third annual cycle of the internal service level agreements is presently under way.

Customer Involvement: The distribution of a corporate customer care guide to all staff was accompanied by an intensive induction and training programme. In addition, the authority took the brave step of engaging MORI, shortly after its establishment in 1996, to assess public perceptions of its services and general performance. A repeat exercise carried out in mid-1998 recorded measured and genuine improvements on levels of satisfaction across almost all areas of service delivery and customer care. Further biannual polls are planned with the aim of both identifying weaknesses and establishing whether continuous improvement across all service areas is being achieved.

Employee Evaluation: Through the Investors In People initiative, the one-to-one achievement and development interviews allow staff at all levels of the organisation to comment openly on the strengths and weaknesses of the service performance. Monthly team briefings, which are also carried out throughout the organisation, also serve to highlight problem areas for management's consideration and action.

The Whole-Authority Approach

Torfaen's original Best Value pilot study submission was based on a 'whole-authority' approach. In doing so, it was proposed that the whole organisation would aim to work within a Best Value framework and would be subject to the challenges and disciplines of the Best Value regime.

In undertaking the first round of reviews in both the DETR and the Welsh Office Evaluation Studies, it was proposed to review 21 services. This represented approximately one-fifth of the council's budget. By selecting at least one service from each of the authority's departments, the opportunities for innovation, learning and sharing experiences throughout the whole organisation were expected to be maximised during the course of the pilot study.

The council also set out to test the framework of Best Value itself by posing a number of fundamental questions, including:

• Does a whole-authority approach to Best Value work in terms of improving performance in all service areas?

• Can Best Value provide an effective overall framework within which to integrate a variety of management and organisational processes, that is, is Best Value the organising framework or is it simply another management tool?

• What are the implications of Best Value, within a whole-authority approach for: innovation in service delivery; achieving demonstrable competitiveness; staffing; relationships with customers; the role and engagement of members; internal and external audit?

• What contribution, if any, can Best Value make to the modernisation of local government, generally?

As the phase I reviews are completed we hope to be able to enlighten these, and other associated questions, and collate the views of all those involved in the process.

DEVELOPING THE PERFORMANCE PLANS

Once the council's pilot bids had been accepted by the Welsh Office and the DETR, it set about preparing its phase I performance plan. Whilst the Best Value committee and the project board guided and monitored the process, the preparation of the individual service plans was delegated to the focus group. In order to engender a common understanding of the evolving process and the different components of Best Value, the project board arranged a series of separate away days for the corporate management team and the focus group. Separate information sessions were also arranged for the Best Value committee and the focus group on specialist subject areas, including communication, partnering, competition, consultation and customer surveys.

The tight timescale of the performance plan preparation period, coupled with other competing demands within the authority's agenda of change, not surprisingly, generated evidence of organisational strain, particularly on the focus group members. The frustration which emanated over the somewhat blurred and continuously evolving agenda of Best Value and the urgency associated with the completion of the phase I plans posed an enormous challenge to the officers concerned. Nevertheless, out of the frustration and internal debates grew a clearer understanding of the evaluation study process itself. The transition to eventually gaining a common purpose and direction was considered by the project board to be largely attributed to the gradual integration of Best Value into the authority's management and organisational processes.

The final performance plans, which were completed by the end of March 1998, reflected the different approaches and the varying levels of understanding within the individual departments. As such, they contained both strengths and weaknesses. Most plans gave clear information on the key service review issues, including methodology, timescales and accountabilities. Some, however, failed to address adequately the issues of demonstrable competitiveness, equalities, the Welsh language and the identification of relevant service performance indicators. Whilst these weaknesses were subsequently attended to during the early part of the service reviews, the different approaches and resulting varying quality of the performance plans were considered to be an inevitable facet of the whole-authority approach. The continuously evolving learning process undoubtedly assisted in broadening the levels of understanding and in securing commitment across all departments.

MANAGING THE SERVICE REVIEWS

Immediately following the submission of the performance plans to the Welsh Office at the end of March 1998, and prior to embarking in earnest on the service reviews, the focus group allowed itself a brief but well-deserved respite. The intensity of the performance plans preparation process had, regrettably, drawn review managers away from some elements of their routine service delivery roles. As such, the completion of the performance plans provided the service review managers an opportunity to return to their respective service delivery routines at the expense of injecting the necessary impetus into the Best Value reviews. Nevertheless, within a few weeks, most departments returned to the serious business of carrying out the service reviews.

In light of a number of competing pressures and of the extent of their respective service review programmes, two departments acquired specialist short-term consulting support to assist in carrying out their reviews. These departments also benefited from these arrangements through the adoption of greater objectivity into the challenge and competition processes of their reviews than experienced elsewhere across the authority.

The authority's 21 phase I service reviews were largely completed by the end of November 1998. The unevenness of approach witnessed in preparing the performance plans appears to have been replicated in the service reviews. Most departments achieved creditable progress within the restricted timescale, in undertaking two of the 4C's of Best Value (Welsh Office, 1998), namely consultation and comparison. However, and in common with a majority of pilot authorities, many service review managers demonstrated reluctance in incorporating the challenge and competition elements of Best Value to the levels suggested in the White Paper guidelines.

It was always anticipated that service managers would find it particularly difficult to take a sufficiently impartial view of challenging why and how their services should be performed. The Project Board attempted to address this weakness by requiring each director to present a broad range of service delivery options to their respective committees for critical consideration.

The second problem area experienced was that of competition, or rather the lack of a real appreciation of how the principles of demonstrable competitiveness should be applied to local authority services. The Welsh Office/Welsh Local Government Association (WLGA) Best Value Project Group strongly encouraged local authorities to explore innovative alternatives to market testing which could pass the test of demonstrable competitiveness. The White Paper, however, simultaneously provided opportunities for disinclined authorities to make use of benchmarking as a credible alternative to competition rather than genuine market testing through competition itself. The inevitable and somewhat disappointing result has been that the majority of local authorities have warmly courted the more politically acceptable yet managerially cumbersome benchmarking option rather than the more radical and effective competition route.

Under CCT, the principles and boundaries of competition were clear. The regulations allowed local authorities little choice and limited room for manoeuvre. Under Best Value, however, the government is encouraging local authorities to abandon their traditional hostility to enforced competition and to use the market enthusiastically as an essential process to improving quality and achieving value for money. Whilst this approach appears to be less prescriptive than CCT, the government may well find it necessary, in the face of increasing reluctance to adopt competition seriously, to adopt a more rigid approach to competition under Best Value.

The issue of demonstrable competitiveness is undoubtedly becoming the most difficult component of Best Value for local authorities to come to terms with and to address satisfactorily. Torfaen adopted a thorough and inclusive process in determining its approach to incorporating demonstrable competitiveness within the Best Value Pilot Scheme. Initial detailed consideration was given by the corporate management team. This was further developed by the elected members at a specific Best Value policy day. The process involved establishing clear guiding principles across all 21 phase I service review areas, irrespective of their previous performance or experience of competition. The guidelines included a commitment to developing methods for achieving demonstrable competitiveness which involved a willingness to tender voluntarily and the use of other appropriate methodologies such as maintaining multiple suppliers and having flexible means to meet peaks and troughs, either in-house or via the market. The key principles included:

- Applying rigorous performance management processes and tests of competitiveness to all services;

- Examining the potential value that exposure to competition provides to a service as a means of determining appropriate tests of competitiveness;

- Where internal processes fail to remedy under-performance, the market will be used to effect service improvement;

- Applying partial or periodic exposure of a service to competition, where there is a well developed market;

- The use of Best Value contracts, without the constraints of CCT. These would focus, in addition to price, on the essential Best Value components of quality, consultation, continuous improvement and flexibility. Such arrangements could be facilitated through mutually beneficial partnerships rather than more adversarial traditional contracting processes.

Not surprisingly, the term flexibility, as it relates to staff, prompted the trade unions to enter the 'demonstrable competitiveness' debate. They viewed the introduction of the term 'flexibility' as a threat to traditional local government employment practices, having the potential to undermine seriously the conditions of employment of their members. The authority however, remained clear in its view that Best Value's primary objective is to meet the needs of citizens and service users. In retaining its commitment to being a good and fair employer, whilst simultaneously applying the principles of competitiveness within Best Value, the authority would incorporate measures to cushion the effects of change by protecting staff, wherever possible. This would be achieved through extensive consultation, training, identifying opportunities for suitable alternative employment and through the application of detriment schemes, where considered appropriate.

The authority also faced some difficulty in meeting the demanding and somewhat inflexible pilot study timescales, which were set by both the DETR and the Welsh Office. The dramatic changes to the traditional political culture needed, above all, space and time. For the radical concepts of Best Value to be willingly adopted by local government, elected members and officers needed a period of acclimatisation to gain a clear understanding of the issues. In particular, the process of transforming an authority from one of resisting competition, as was largely the case under CCT, to one of warmly embracing demonstrable competitiveness, under Best Value, cannot be achieved overnight or through a single policy meeting. Whilst local authorities are generally wholeheartedly committed to Best Value, if the initiative is to succeed, the facilitators of its implementation, particularly elected members and staff, need to be comfortable with the process within an acceptable and workable timescale.

The introduction of Best Value has also placed a number of additional new challenges on the authority. The traditional, introverted, top-down hierarchical management styles of senior managers are gradually being opened up within the corporate desire to allow all staff to gain a clear understanding of the new initiative. Commitment to continuous improvement and opportunities for innovation cannot occur without a thorough understanding of the concept throughout the whole organisation. In order to achieve this corporate understanding, Torfaen is actively promoting a fifth 'C' of Best Value – communication – as an internal marketing exercise for ensuring that managers place the necessary emphasis on developing and monitoring more effective internal communication channels throughout.

In terms of managing the Best Value pilot scheme internally, the service review lead officers are becoming increasingly frustrated with the complexities of the reporting and monitoring processes with which they are having to comply. Internally, periodic reports are required for departmental team meetings, corporate management team, service committees and the Best Value Committee. Furthermore, in addition to the overall objective of providing detailed service reviews and action plans, the pilot scheme evaluators, Cardiff Business School, require periodic self-evaluation reports, and the study monitors, District Audit, require verification of all information and data associated with the foregoing processes throughout the duration of the exercise. In Torfaen there are the added requirements of the DETR study by Warwick Business School. Nevertheless, in spite of the plethora of recording, evaluation and monitoring processes associated with the Best Value pilot studies, there remains a strong and positive commitment within the authority to make the initiative work. The vast majority of elected members and staff at all levels view Best Value as a most timely and welcome measure, and are prepared to put up with the administrative burdens inherent within the Pilot Scheme, in the interests of the oft-repeated adage – 'No pain – No gain'!

A DEPARTMENTAL PERSPECTIVE

This section focuses on a practitioner's view of the Best Value initiative. We have discussed the corporate framework for the management of Best Value and in this section we now explain the management processes within the environmental management department of Torfaen County Borough Council.

The environmental management department is essentially a marriage of traditional district council technical services and environmental health departments with the highways, transportation and trading standards functions inherited from the Gwent County Council on reorganisation. This mix of services was unique in Wales at the time of reorganisation; however, Monmouthshire County Council now has a similar structure.

Many of the staff forming the department were experienced in market testing. The department has the client functions for highways maintenance (1980 Act) and grounds maintenance, refuse and cleansing services (1988 Act). It undertakes highways, drainage and general municipal engineering capital projects and manages the select list of contractors for the council as a whole. Furthermore, an engineering consultancy section was established in the department at reorganisation in anticipation of CCT for the defined activity of 'construction and property related services'.

The department also inherited staff with experience in quality management: a number of staff were qualified lead assessors. Highway engineers from Gwent County Council were able to transfer the ISO 9001 quality system to the unitary authority with the agreement of Lloyds Quality Assurance subject to audit. The need to prepare the in-house consultancy for competition also provided the incentive to introduce a computerised time management and project management system and to develop scale fees and project costing for internal service level agreements and a small amount of work undertaken for other public bodies. The senior manager responsible for the consultancy also produced a business plan for the first time in April 1998. In parts of the department it can be seen, therefore, that performance management was an everyday reality, albeit without the rigour and breadth of the Best Value regime. However, Best Value required a strengthening and broadening of what already existed rather than a fundamental shift in culture.

Once the decision had been taken to pilot Best Value on a whole-authority basis, each department was asked to put forward two or three services for first-phase performance reviews. The director, following consultation with the staff involved, put forward housing grants, grounds maintenance and the work of the traffic and development team for first-phase review. Housing grants were chosen particularly as the department provides an agency service for those successful in their applications for grant and the director was concerned about the lack of performance measures in place both relating to the work load of surveyors and the 'profitability' of the team. Problems with budgetary control had also been experienced. The grants agency team, with the enthusiastic support of its members, had been identified as a pilot for process benchmarking prior to the 1997 general election. The grounds maintenance service was chosen because it had been decided to create a comprehensive service for the council, which, amongst other things, required transfer of staff from another department and the preparation of a new contract specification. The traffic and development team were chosen particularly because of concern about performance in street lighting.

The environmental management department was also a leader in the development of annual service planning. The third service and organisational development plan was produced in April 1998 and covers the financial year 1998/99. The involvement of staff in the development of objectives for the plan was also in line with principle of Best Value relating to staff consultation on service delivery and performance.

Whilst the framework described above was good preparation for the Best Value initiative, much more was required, as will be described. Whilst there were some areas of good practice in the department, it was necessary to ensure that performance management techniques were more widely understood and utilised. The first task was to decide how the initiative would be managed within the department. The director was a member of the Best Value project board and the assistant director (engineering services) represented the department on the Best Value focus group. Therefore, representation and involvement at a corporate level was good. It was necessary, however, to establish structures within the department which would enable the range of professional disciplines and a range of junior to senior staff to be involved. The approach taken was to form four departmental working groups as illustrated in Figure 2. All of the staff, in groups of around 25, were given a presentation on Best Value by the assistant director and director. At the end of each session staff were invited to complete a simple questionnaire using 'smiley faces' to test their understanding of the concept and their level of personal commitment. The results were very encouraging, as will be seen from Figure 3. Subsequently staff were invited by memorandum to volunteer to sit on one of the departmental working groups. The number of volunteers was less than the number who had expressed themselves willing when they completed the questionnaire, nevertheless there were sufficient for the groups to operate. In order to ensure that the work of the groups was relevant and supportive to the first phase review services a joint training session for members of the groups and staff involved in first phase reviews was held in May 1998.

One of the advantages of effective corporate management in a local authority is that departments can assist each other, addressing strengths and weaknesses and sharing best practice. This is only really effective when there is a spirit of trust. No one would be ready to acknowledge weaknesses if the response were to be punitive or even if a colleague was to take advantage of the situation. Torfaen has a very supportive corporate management team and Best Value has provided many opportunities for co-operation. The performance plans produced by the environmental management department for the first-phase reviews were made available to other departments as a possible model. The director made presentations on performance plans and process benchmarking to meetings of the Best Value Committee and contributed to the 'front end' of the council's performance plan document. He was responsible for preparing a paper on 'demonstrable competitiveness' for consideration by the corporate management team. He also attended a social services department training day as an 'expert' in process benchmarking. A number of staff from other departments together with external specialists were available to syndicate groups set up on the

FIGURE 1

BEST VALUE ORGANISATIONAL FRAMEWORK

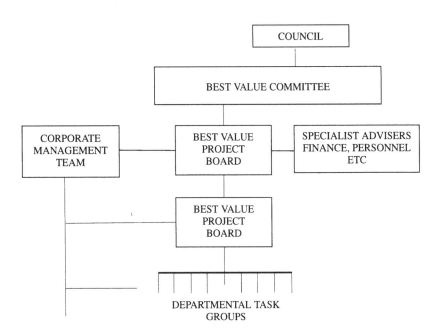

FIGURE 2

DEPARTMENTAL BEST VALUE FRAMEWORK

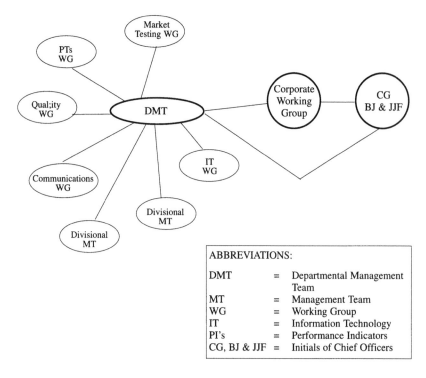

FIGURE 3

BEST VALUE – DISCUSSION WITH STAFF FEB'98 – FEEDBACK
(Numbers relate to staff returning forms at Feedback Sessions)

	😊	😐	🙁	☹️
1. Do you understand what is meant by Best Value?	61	32	1	1
2. Do you think you can contribute to Best Value?	52	36	3	4
3. Do you think you can see how Best Value may relate to your own work?	43	42	10	0
4. Would you be interested in contributing to the Departmental Topic Groups?	37	21	26	21

training day should they have needed advice in areas of performance management. Senior staff of the department have been made available to advise other departments on quality systems, customer surveys, project management and process benchmarking.

A FOCUS ON TOOLS AND TECHNIQUES

Reference was made in the previous section to some of the performance management tools and techniques in use in Torfaen. We will examine some of these in more detail, again using the experiences of the environmental management department by way of illustration.

Service Planning

Torfaen has been developing and refining its service planning processes since the requirement on reorganisation for each Welsh unitary authority to produce a service delivery plan. Whilst it was no longer a statutory requirement of the councils to produce a service delivery plan after the first year, Torfaen decided to continue to produce plans whilst aiming to improve the process of consultation with the public and the reporting of service targets and performance. The plan, now known as the community and performance plan to reflect the change in emphasis, forms the head of the planning hierarchy, as illustrated in Figure 4. It contains broad objectives within generic topic areas rather than mirroring exactly the departmental structure.

Department service plans form the next level of the planning hierarchy. The environmental management department's plan contains a statement of the accountabilities of the departmental management team – a kind of corporate job description. This is followed by a section for each team which lists the members of the team, accountabilities, an account of performance in the previous year against performance indicators where they exist, service targets and organisational development targets. A departmental A–Z completes the plan. Whilst its primary purpose is for internal management, it is copied to members who are able to use it for reference purposes. Targets in the plan are endorsed by the environmental management committee, which also receives a report on performance at the end of the financial year.

The targets in the plan are developed in team meetings and participation of all members of each team is encouraged. Senior managers review the draft targets and revised targets are negotiated if necessary. When the plan is completed (April) the targets in schedule form are put on the departmental server and are therefore accessible to all staff. The schedules should be updated monthly for a report to the departmental management team. The record for the completed month is then archived and made read-only. This

FIGURE 4

PLANNING HIERARCHY

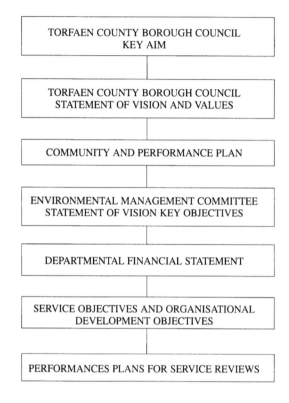

process was new to the staff of the department on reorganisation and a number of teams were over-optimistic in setting targets. Furthermore, some teams were more disciplined in their performance monitoring than others, discussing performance at monthly team meetings and keeping schedules updated. The targets for the 1998/99 plan were produced in the light of two year's experience and were considered to be both challenging and achievable. Targets would cover such matters as the introduction of new systems by a particular date and the percentage of food premises inspected. Performance monitoring and reporting has improved but there is still much room for improvement. A new element of the procedure is to require each team to undertake a formal mid-financial year review of performance in November and to report to the departmental management team. At the same review meeting, each team will commence discussion of the proposed targets for the following year.

Process Benchmarking

The director of environmental management began discussions about process benchmarking with the council's audit manager from District Audit. However little progress was made until the autumn of 1997 by which time it had become clear that process benchmarking would play an important role in the Best Value regime. In fact, with an effective and experienced facilitator, the use of process benchmarking can ensure that performance review is thorough and comprehensive. It was agreed that Torfaen would take the lead in inviting local authorities to participate in the club, in providing a venue and administrative support. District Audit agreed to facilitate the meetings, advise on the validity of data and establish a database of authorities and performance indicators. A decision was taken to run two clubs back to back for (i) administration of housing grants and (ii) housing grants agency (a consultancy service to grants applicants operated as a business unit). Four Welsh authorities and two English authorities agreed to join the club. Whilst it was most probable that this small sample would not include the best practice authority in England and Wales, the intention was to develop a set of key performance indicators which a wider group of authorities would be invited to use. This wider group would be based on the Audit Commission family authorities of club members.

At the first meeting of the clubs the audit manager, with two colleagues, gave an explanation of the technique of process benchmarking. Following this the groups broke into the two clubs which spent most of the day discussing and agreeing critical success factors and key performance indicators for their services. At the following meeting they were to return with a process map and their performance indicators. The process mapping created little difficulty, although some authorities provided the information in flow chart form and others in textual form. However, there were considerable difficulties with the performance indicators. It became clear that there were two main problems; first the definition of the indicators had not been sufficiently precise and, secondly, the financial management information available to the officers was in some cases very poor. This is also a problem for the citizen's charter performance indicators, but it is less apparent as practitioners tend not to share detailed information on the data which underpins the national indicators. It was relatively easy to redefine the performance indicators, but it will take time and tenacity to realise the improvements to financial management information systems.

The indicators that are now being shared, together with the process maps, give the best guide at present to relative efficiency and effectiveness and some clues to how to improve. The same comments apply to the benchmarking club for grounds maintenance which has a membership of

TABLE 1

KEY INDICATORS FROM BENCHMARKING EXERCISE

Groups Maintenance	Housing Grants
Urban grass annual cost/hectare	Number of grants processed/person/annum
Urban grass cost/head	Time from approval to completion
Bowling green annual cost	% of unforeseen works
Bowling green cost/user	Average value of grants
Annual cost soccer pitch	Staff costs as a % expenditure on grants
Soccer pitch cost/user	Satisfaction with council administration
Rugby pitch cost/user	Satisfaction with contractor

nine Welsh authorities and commenced work in April 1998. Details of these key performance indicators are given in the department's action plans produced at the end of the Best Value service reviews. Some of the key indicators from both benchmarking exercises are shown in Table 1.

One further important factor is the agreement to design common customer satisfaction questionnaires. The benefit will be that inter-authority comparison of cost-effectiveness and customer satisfaction will be possible. The result will provide a new dimension for Best Value, that is, lowest cost with highest customer satisfaction. The district audit manager now aims to invite other authorities to use the same performance indicators for housing grants and for grounds maintenance in an enlarged database. As for expanding this work, arrangements are being made at the end of 1998 to create a number of further clubs to cover technical services functions. Again these will be facilitated by District Audit. Although Welsh-based, a number of English authorities are expressing interest in this benchmarking activity. It will certainly be possible for these authorities to exchange data for the key performance indicators and it may be possible to invite some of them to participate as full club members.

CONCLUSION

It may be a little premature to draw categoric and firm conclusions from the processes which were adopted and from the lessons learned in participating in phase I of the Welsh Office and DETR Best Value evaluation studies.

The whole-authority approach was deliberately adopted from the outset to encourage all departments to work within a Best Value framework. Torfaen set itself a particularly demanding agenda in reviewing 21 of its services. Early indications suggest the corporate approach to the initiative, which links closely to developing community planning and performance management processes, and which is supported by an extensive communications framework, has allowed the organisation to gain a broad understanding of the new concept. The sharing of experiences and continuous learning processes inherent within a whole-authority approach have undoubtedly assisted in stimulating a genuine commitment to Best Value as well as in rousing a new culture of change throughout.

The timely introduction of the 4C's as a guiding mechanism proved invaluable in developing a clear methodology for carrying out service reviews. Service review managers appeared comfortable with and achieved good early progress in consulting on and in comparing services. However, serious difficulties were experienced in coming to terms with and in applying the challenge and competition components of Best Value. Service managers, quite understandably, demonstrated a nervousness in openly challenging their services. Arising from these difficulties, it is likely greater use of independent facilitators or the adoption of the business excellence model will be encouraged in the phase II reviews.

Whereas the government has promoted market testing as the favoured means of demonstrating competitiveness, local authorities generally have focused their attentions primarily on benchmarking during phase I. In Torfaen, the inclusive process in determining the approach to demonstrable competitiveness resulted in a broad and mixed economy of benchmarking, internal restructuring, market testing by means of partial and full competition as well as through more innovative partnering contracts. It is likely, as the council moves into phase II it will explore further opportunities to take advantage of partnership sourcing within less formal contractual arrangements in selected areas.

However, the critical issue of demonstrable competitiveness remains the Achilles' heel of Best Value. Whereas local authorities, generally, have enthusiastically welcomed the replacement of CCT with Best Value, there appears to be a determined reluctance to embrace competition as an essential component of Best Value. If local authorities continue deliberately to circumvent competition by pursuing benchmarking and performance indicators for demonstrating competitiveness, Best Value will not be achieved. In the final analysis, if the government perceives that local government is incapable of securing demonstrable competitiveness through its favoured means, it is inevitable that secondary legislation will include a compulsion to incorporate open competition within the Best Value framework.

REFERENCES

Armstrong, Rt Hon Hilary, 1997, Minister for Local Government, 'The 12 Principles of Best Value' (2 June).
Beecham, Sir Jeremy, 1998, *Municipal Journal*, 5 Dec.

Local Government (Wales) Act 1994: Enacting Local Government Reorganisation in Wales (1996).

Torfaen County Borough Council's Best Value Pilot Scheme Performance Plans (April 1998).

Welsh Office/WLGA, 1997, Report of the Joint Best Value Project Group entitled 'A Framework for Developing Best Value in Welsh Local Government' (August).

Welsh Office, 1998, Consultation Paper: Modernising Local Government in Wales – 'Improving Services Through Best Value' (April).

Notes on Contributors

Dean Bartlett *et al.* are in the School of Law at the University of North London.

George Boyne is Professor of Public Sector Management and co-ordinator of the Public Services Research Unit at Cardiff Business School, Cardiff University.

Howard Davis is a Lecturer in the Local Government Centre at Warwick Business School, The University of Warwick.

Julian Gould-Williams is a Researcher in the Public Services Research Unit at Cardiff Business School, Cardiff University.

Joseph Field is Director of Environmental Management with Torfaen County Borough.

Brian James is Best Value Project Manager with Torfaen County Borough.

Jennifer Law is a Principal Lecturer in the Business School at the University of Glamorgan.

Neil McGarvey is a Lecturer in Politics in the Department of Government at the University of Strathclyde.

Steve Martin is a Principal Research Fellow in the Local Government Centre at Warwick Business School, The University of Warwick.

Arthur Midwinter is Dean of the Faculty of Arts and Social Sciences at the University of Strathclyde.

John Wilson is a Principal Lecturer in Public Service Management at Liverpool Business School, Liverpool John Moores University.

Bruce Walker is a Senior Lecturer in the Institute of Local Government Studies at The University of Birmingham where he specialises in research into contracting and social housing finance.

Richard Walker is a Senior Lecturer in the Department of City and Regional Planning at Cardiff University.

Index

www.ingramcontent.com/pod-product-compliance
Ingram Content Group UK Ltd.
Pitfield, Milton Keynes, MK11 3LW, UK
UKHW041839280225
455677UK00010B/251